Wounds of Deception

PATRICE TARTT

Wounds of Deception is a work of fiction and does not depict any actual person or event. Although events may be inspired in part by incidents that may or may not have been experienced by certain members of the general population, the events within this book are entirely fictional. Unless an individual is explicitly identified by name, the statements used should not be directly attributed to any specific person. Similarly, the storyline is also purely fiction. Names, characters, places, and incidents are products of the author's imagination or are used fictitiously and are not to be construed as real. Any resemblance to actual events, locales or organizations, or persons, living or dead is entirely coincidental.

Copyright 2013 by Patrice Tartt
Published by Patrice Tartt Publishing, LLC

All rights reserved. Printed in the United States of America. No part of this book may be used, reproduced, stored in or introduced into a retrieval system, or transmitted in any form or by any means (electronic, mechanical, by photocopying, recording or otherwise) without written permission from the author.

The scanning, uploading, and distribution of this book via the Internet or by any other means without the permission of the author is illegal and punishable by law. Please purchase only authorized printed or electronic editions and do not participate in or encourage electronic piracy of copyrighted materials. The author appreciates your support of authors' rights.

ISBN 13: 9780615847610
ISBN: 0615847617
Library of Congress Control Number: 2013914545
Patrice Tartt, Woodbridge, VA

Library of Congress Cataloging-In-Publication Data
Cover design by Dashawn Taylor
Please visit the author's website and social media pages to stay connected with the author and to purchase additional copies:
www.patricetartt.com
Twitter.com/PatriceTartt
Facebook.com/AuthorPatriceTartt
If you are a member of a book club, please visit the book club page on the website for discussion questions and more information on connecting your club with the author.

Dedication
I dedicate this book to my loving parents and beautiful son. To my beloved father and angel, I miss and love you dearly.
Mr. Grady Tartt
September 17, 1941-April 2, 2011
For God so loved the world that he gave his one and only Son, that whoever **believes** *in him shall not* **perish** *but have* **eternal life.**

John 3:16

"Wounds of Deception is a must read. It is a powerful and riveting book about family relationship challenges after the loss of a family member. This book educates and advocates while raising awareness on seldom discussed topics."

Mary E. O'Donnell, President of the Amyloidosis Foundation (amyloidosis.org)

Foreword

Betrayal and financial exploitation are often difficult to accept and overcome. The challenge of recovering from the violation of one's spirit is uniquely severe when it results from the callous actions of a caregiver, trusted neighbor, friend or family member. The simultaneous loss of a loved one makes the road to emotional recovery particularly arduous. In *Wounds of Deception*, Patrice Tartt tells a cautionary tale of the temptation of money and the high price that may be paid —emotionally and financially--when the people you love and care about most, place their own selfish and immoral interests ahead of the interests of those they are entrusted with protecting. Although a work of fiction, *Wounds of Deception* sadly is based on true stories of insidious financial exploitation and an egregious violation of trust that has happened to many people after the death of a loved one.

The book you are about to read paints a portrait of greed, narcissism and neglect. However, that's just the beginning of the story! *Wounds of Deception* is ultimately a book about love, hope, courage, redemption and self-respect. The book tells an engaging story of determination and resilience in the face of personal loss and financial and emotional devastation. When you finish this book, you'll be mindful of the inevitabilities of life and determined to prepare yourself and those you love for an uncertain future.

Reading *Wounds of Deception* reminded me that, despite the fact that I'm an immigration attorney, I'm often asked questions about wills and trusts. My standard response to such inquiries is, *"Please see an experienced trusts and estates attorney."* This book is worth reading because not only is it entertaining, it reminds me of the importance of having adequate life insurance and of keeping ones families in the information loop regarding the location of vital personal documents and financial records. (I can recommend a fire-proof home safe for storage of the aforementioned documents.) I also believe that it's particularly important that you maintain a document or electronic file (such as a flash drive) for a **_trusted_** family member, which identifies information about your bank accounts and other financial assets and liabilities. The document should also contain the passwords to your credit cards, debit cards, computers, iPads, mobile devices and every other password-protected gadget that you own.

I sincerely recommend *Wounds of Deception*. I am confident that the book will confirm the power of faith and hope in healing the emotional scars caused by deception, exploitation and egregious breaches of trust. In addition to reminding you to be vigilant when entrusting your finances and medical care to those closest to you, this book will also motivate and inspire you to maintain your resolve in the face of heartbreak and adversity—no matter the cause. After you have read *Wounds of Deception*, I hope that you will be mindful, yet again, of the poetic and prophetic words of Maya Angelou:

> *You may shoot me with your words,*
> *You may cut me with your eyes,*
> *You may kill me with your hatefulness,*
> *But still, like air, I'll rise.*

James Bond, Esq.
San Diego, California (2013)

Acknowledgements

First, I want to give all praise and thanks to God for instilling the dream and vision within me to write my debut novel. Without him, my dream would have never come to fruition. He is the main reason why I was able to stay committed and dedicated to this project and I am forever thankful.

To my son, you have been my inspiration and I thank you for allowing me to split my time with you and writing, it will definitely pay off in the end. All the late nights and long hours that I have put in to make sure that I have a quality story to share with the world, and you allowed me to do this by being the best little boy that any mommy could ask for. I love you with all my heart, and if I have anything to do with it, you will always have everything that you need and never want for anything.

To my dad, I know that you are in Heaven watching over me and your first grandchild. You are the reason why I wrote this book, and I can say with much confidence that I am continuing to make you proud. Writing this book has been extremely challenging and time consuming, and you gave me the strength to continue and see it through. I miss you and I love you dearly.

To my mom, my number one fan and cheerleader, where would I be in life without you? You have instilled in me everything that I need to be the successful woman that I am today. Thank you for all of your advice, ideas and suggestions pertaining to my book. The older that I get the more I become like you. Thank you for your encouragement, support and prayers. I love you always.

To my friend Zelda Corona, all of the phone calls, emails and text messages to you ALL the time asking for your advice and suggestions, thank you! I'm not sure what I would have done without you during this process. I can now say that not only are you a good friend of mine, but also a fellow author. I thank you for your encouragement, support and prayers. Love you.

To Gary Davis & Michelle Fuselier, thank you all for everything. The two of you are simply the best. It has been wonderful knowing both of you for the past four years and no matter what advice you all give, it is always on time. I am so thankful to have met the two of you and I look forward to more laughs, advice and inspiration from you both. Love you all.

Thank you to everyone who provided support, prayers and encouragement during my writing journey. It is greatly appreciated and will never be forgotten.

Patrice Tartt

Introduction

Wounds of Deception is a novel that will have you questioning who you can actually trust. Whether it is friends or family, it is always good to know who is for you and who is against you.

After the unexpected death of my father in 2011, I was completely devastated. Three months prior, my son was born and many said that he resembled my father. I couldn't see the resemblance at first, but the older that he gets, the more he becomes a spitting image of my father. Unfortunately, my father never got the opportunity to meet his one and only grandchild, because we lived in different states and my son was only three weeks old and too young to travel with me to see him. To this day, I show my son pictures of my father and say "g'papi," and he repeats it. It is the cutest thing ever to hear him say that.

The day of my father's funeral, I stood outside of his house and said out loud that I was going to write a book and I am so proud to say that my dream came to fruition. My debut novel covers so many topics that most people don't want to talk about. It is time to break the silence and discuss these things because death is something that we cannot avoid. When a loved one experiences an illness or we experience the death of a loved one, we must be prepared and know who we can trust to be Power of Attorney and handle all financial matters. It is never too early or too late to properly plan for an unexpected illness or death. An excellent medical doctor to properly diagnose any illnesses in advance, along with an experienced financial advisor, trusts and estates attorney, and last but not least, a well thought out living-will and long-term care plan are all necessities. If you have not considered them already, these things should be on your list of priorities in the event the unexpected should occur.

The power of prayer is simply amazing, and knowing God along with trusting and believing in him, is even better. In order to cope with a loss and especially an unexpected loss is to continue to pray and know that God makes no mistakes. Two years later, sometimes I still cannot believe that my father is no longer here with us, but having a good support system is what it takes to stay strong.

I invite you to sit back, relax, and enjoy my debut novel *Wounds of Deception*, which I wrote with much passion and motivation. The topics covered are seldom talked about, but I feel it's time we break the silence on these issues.

Prologue

Two Years Earlier

"Kenneth, stop playing so much!" Christie heard someone yell as she closed her car door and stepped into the warm sun. She didn't need to look over and see what kind of mischief her father had gotten into because he was a natural prankster and the life of the party.

"I'm not doing anything," Christie heard him say as she slowly turned around and saw him tiptoeing towards her.

"Daddy?" Christie said with a sly grin on her face, "What on earth are you up to now?"

As soon as her father got close enough, he chuckled, placed his lanky arm around her shoulder, and pulled her in for a hug.

"Baby girl, why do you always have to think your daddy's up to no good?" he asked as he leaned over and pecked her cheek lightly.

Christie laughed and shook her head. She knew her father well enough to know that whatever he was up to would soon be revealed.

"How was your drive?" Kenneth asked as he took his eyes off the large gathering of people at the picnic shed.

Christie shrugged and took a deep breath, "Long, as usual. But I'm glad to see you. Glad to be here."

Kenneth grinned widely, showing all of his pearly whites and a dimple on the right cheek. "All your cousins have been asking when you were going to get here. You would think they were waiting on Oprah the way they kept checking the parking lot," he said with a wink.

"Hey, hey!" Christie said as she poked him jokingly in the side, "I'm Oprah to somebody."

Kenneth playfully dodged Christie's poking and pulled her back into a tight hug.

"You know you are your daddy's Oprah. You're my superstar, baby girl," he said as he planted a long kiss on her forehead and started walking towards the shed where the music, laughter, and glorious smells were coming from.

Christie loved her father and he undeniably loved her back. Looking at the two of them was almost like seeing double but you would never get the two of them to agree to that statement. Their skin resembled a perfectly toasted almond. While Kenneth had a smile that could charm a rattlesnake, Christie had a sparkle in her eye that would make that same rattlesnake blush. As a child, Christie would stare at her handsome father for hours on end trying to find the similitude between them. He was tall, a tad lanky and always kept a neat haircut. His piercing eyes were light brown like small pools of honey that made you feel like he could see straight through to a person's soul in once glance. Yet Christie on the other hand, was curvy without being overweight and of average height for a woman, yet not as tall as her father. Her hazel eyes drew people into her every time. Still, in every other way they were almost identical.

"You have my nose and my eye shape," Kenneth said one day while Christie sat Indian-style on the living room floor of his apartment playing with her Barbie doll. She usually spent her weekends with her father, and whenever he addressed her, she listened intensely to every word he said.

"That's all?" Christie asked with a pinch of disappointment in her voice.

Kenneth picked her chin up with his perfectly manicured fingers and smiled widely "And you have my smile and my eyebrows and guess what else?" Kenneth asked playfully as Christie jolted up with excitement.

"We even have the same pinkies."

Christie furrowed her eyebrows and cocked her head back.

"Pinkies, Daddy?" she asked examining her hands and quickly looking back at her father's hand.

Without missing a beat, Kenneth knelt beside the confused Christie and placed her hand beside his. Christie stared at the two hands—one larger and one smaller, one rough and one smooth—and squinted her eyes.

"See here?" Kenneth asked as he traced his free hand along the edge of his daughter's pinky, pointing out the way her finger shifted slightly to the right.

"Mine does that same thing," he said as he pointed to his own right-shifting pinky.

Christie's eyes lit up. "I see it!"

"That's so cool, Daddy!" she said with a gasp as she wrapped her hands around his neck and squeezed tightly.

That night when Kenneth tucked her into bed, Christie grabbed his hand as he prepared to leave the room and pushed her pinky up to his. From that night on, that was their "thing". Many years later, as Christie approached her thirties, it still was.

"Now listen," said her father as they walked slowly towards the picnic shed where the red and white *Whitfield Family Reunion* sign hung, "your aunt has no idea but—"

"KENNETH!" Christie heard her Aunt Angelica yell loudly,

"I'm going to hurt you!"

Christie started laughing before she even knew what was going on.

"Kenneth, I promise you—oh, Christie, my favorite niece! How are you, darling?" Angelica said excitedly as she realized who her brother was talking to and hugging.

"Hey, Auntie!" Christie said as she broke from her father's hug and embraced her aunt.

Aunt Angelica was one of the cutest women Christie had ever had the pleasure of seeing. Her Halle Berry-esque haircut and adorable button nose always captivated Christie's attention. Christie was aware of her aunt's beauty and it seemed, so was the rest of the world. With her cute nose, clear skin and fit body, Angelica was gorgeous. Like Kenneth's, Angelica had also inherited the piercing eyes.

"Your father is something else." Angelica said as she gently hit him on the shoulder.

"What did he do this time?" Christie asked as she raised an eyebrow and crossed her arms.

Kenneth's hands shot heavenward as he shook his head and grinned. "I'm innocent!"

Ignoring his antics, Angelica turned her attention back to Christie.

"Do you know your father—my baby brother—hid all of my potato salad?"

Christie chuckled as she dropped her head and bit her bottom lip. The running joke in their family had always been how disgusting Angelica's potato salad was. Hearing that her father had hidden it was hilarious.

"Christie, are you laughing?" her aunt asked playfully as she inched closer.

Christie shook her head and tried to divert Angelica's attention by pointing at the soaring blue jays in the sky. Her aunt loved them and collected just about anything with a blue jay on it.

"Junior specifically asked me to make my potato salad this year. You know it's been three years since we've had a Whitfield family reunion..."

Christie's eyes lit up at the mention of her cousin's name.

"Junior's here?" she asked as she scanned the crowd, cutting off her aunt.

"He's around here somewhere. I can't keep up with him or Michael."

Christie's relationship with her cousin Junior was more like brother and sister than like cousins. Even though he'd always had a troubled relationship with his mother—even going as far as being estranged from her for three years—Christie knew deep down that he loved her.

"I haven't seen him in so long," Christie said as she looked over and saw her aunt smiling proudly.

"You two were always close. Reminds me so much of how close your dad, Evelyn and I are."

Christie felt her eyes roll slightly and caught herself just as Angelica looked in her direction. It wasn't that Christie didn't love her Aunt Evelyn; it was just that she was a difficult person to *like*. Unlike Angelica, Evelyn was nowhere near as outgoing, friendly or talkative. There had been times when Christie would be in the house all weekend with her father and two aunts and only exchange one word with her Aunt Evelyn. Kenneth had told her a long time ago not to take Evelyn's lack of emotion as a direct insult and Christie had learned to do just that, but it didn't change the fact that she didn't like her aunt all that much.

"Evelyn was just asking about you too," Angelica said with a grin on her face. She knew–everyone was aware that Christie and Evelyn didn't have the best relationship, though they tried to smooth over any friction.

"Oh, was she?" Christie asked sarcastically as her father nudged her and shook his head while he and Angelica giggled to themselves.

"You look good, girl," Angelica said as she looked Christie up and down, nodding in approval. Although Christie would never admit it, Angelica's opinion mattered to her. While she had always had her own mother to look up to and emulate, her Aunt Angelica was a good secondary role model.

"Thanks, Auntie," Christie replied with a wink. She knew she looked good; a far cry from how she'd looked three years earlier. She was now eight years out of college, a newlywed of one year and had totally found herself. Now she stood tall—a shapely woman with confidence, energy and drive. Her caramel skin was lightly bronzed from working many days in the sun as a news reporter, and her hair was cut in a bob with light blonde highlights framing her face. She was no longer the baby girl they were used to seeing tagging along with Kenneth; she was a woman now.

"Where's Anthony?" Angelica asked.

Christie's husband had taken to her family almost immediately. Her father and husband loved debating for hours over books, politics and business news; it had been a relief for Christie. When they had married a year earlier in a big ceremony in Chicago, the city where she was born and raised, Christie prepared herself for the question about grandchildren.

"When are y'all going to try for a baby?" one of Anthony's older aunts asked the day after their wedding as they prepared for their honeymoon in Jamaica.

Christie was strong-minded and knew what she wanted, and that was for her and Anthony to be secure in their careers before introducing another person into their relationship. She just smiled and politely entertained the woman's questions.

"Don't listen to them, babe. You and I know what we want, right?" Anthony asked after his aunt left the room. Christie remembered Anthony's oversized hands pulling her towards him and in that moment everything felt okay. Standing 6" tall, Anthony Adams had the presence to make a room either erupt in laughter or hush in silence. That very quality intrigued Christie when they'd first started dating. Something about him reminded her of her father and as the saying goes, a girl always falls in love with a man who reminds her of her daddy. Anthony fit every aspect of her mental and emotional checklist for a mate and Christie was thankful he had exceeded her physical expectations. With dark brown skin and a dimple in his chin, Anthony's smile was so wide and so white, Christie felt herself falling in love with him every time he grinned. He had always been conscientious about his weight and staying fit and that helped Christie stay focused on it as well. The two were far from bodybuilders but they both enjoyed working out and staying healthy together.

Snapping out of her daydream, Christie remembered her aunt had asked about Anthony's whereabouts.

"He had an expo to attend in Dallas. He tried to cancel it; he really wanted to be here."

"Well, maybe next time," Angelica said.

"And maybe next time you'll have a baby in your arms," Kenneth slipped in with a laugh.

Christie rolled her eyes and shook her head. Her father had made it crystal clear that he wanted grandchildren sooner than later. With Christie being his only child, Kenneth was eager to hear the pitter-patter of little feet running through his heart. Still, Christie and Anthony had only been married a year and they were just getting used to having one another around. They weren't ready for a baby.

"We can only hope Christie blesses us with grandchildren before we're too old to play with them," Christie heard a voice say.

"Ma, what are you doing here?" Christie yelped as she rushed to hug her mother tightly.

Although her mother and father had been divorced for many years, and her mother had remarried four years earlier, the two of them remained on good terms. Unlike some of her friends, Christie had the perfect relationship with *both* her mother and father. There were no tense moments or separate holidays; they truly were one family. When her mother had married Daniel Kelly, Kenneth was even tasked with handing out programs at the ceremony. They were *that* cool with one another and Christie loved it.

"You know your father wasn't going to let me miss out on a Whitfield family reunion, baby," Alise said with excitement in her voice.

"Besides, the last time I had decent barbeque was at my sorority's national convention five years ago and you know how your mother loves barbeque."

"I don't blame you. The Whitfield's can certainly throw down on some barbeque, can't they?" Angelica said.

Alise nodded and placed her hands on her shapely hips. "Now, what was this I overheard about grandbabies? Did I hear you saying we'd have some soon?" Alise asked as she stood shoulder-to-shoulder with Kenneth. If Christie could have contained her smile she would have; but seeing them together, forces joined, made her giggle.

"I didn't mention anything about children, Ma. Anthony and I are not ready for all that right now."

Alise shrugged her shoulders and cleared her throat. "Kenneth, when we had Christie what did we have to our name?" she asked with a raised eyebrow.

"Love and a prayer," Kenneth replied through a muffled laugh.

For once, Christie wished Anthony was there to help block some of the discussion on children; he was perfect for defusing the talk. Christie usually just changed the subject.

"It smells good over there and I'm hungry," Christie said as she smoothed out her white tee shirt and raised her eyebrows.

Kenneth and Alise laughed and knew the change of subject meant the discussion was over.

"Well, I'm going to take that as my cue. Let me go over here and speak to Aunt Ethel," Alise said as she excused herself, "I'll be right back."

"Looks like you haven't missed a meal at all," Christie heard a voice say behind her back. She knew who it was before she turned around.

"Hey, Aunt Evelyn," Christie replied dryly as she slowly turned to face her aunt.

Aunt Evelyn was a nice looking woman, when she was younger; although she was nowhere near as pretty as Angelica. It was her dry, emotionless attitude that kept most people at bay. She had hair falling to her shoulders with flecks of salt and pepper color throughout. Unlike Angelica, Evelyn didn't care too much about being cute and it showed. She had moles on her caramel-colored face and her body looked like it had seen better days. Christie sometimes wondered if Evelyn tried to look unattractive to match her horrible attitude. Even with Christie and Evelyn not being the best of friends, she couldn't deny her aunt had a beautiful smile. While she didn't have the piercing eyes that Kenneth and Angelica had, Evelyn's smile had won her plenty of fanfare. Standing taller than Angelica but shorter than Kenneth, their sister had a presence about her that could not be ignored.

"Evelyn!" Angelica gasped as she shoved her sister slightly, "Christie's not fat."

Evelyn leaned in and lightly hugged her niece, "I didn't say she was fat, Angelica, I said she doesn't look like she's missing any meals. She looks healthy."

Christie gritted her teeth and smiled despite being mad enough to take a swing at her aunt. Her father and Aunt Angelica just shook their heads and stared at Evelyn as if she was crazy.

"My baby girl looks good. I was just telling her that."

Evelyn nodded, "Yeah, you do look good Christie."

Christie was never surprised at how hot and cold her Aunt Evelyn was with her. One moment she was telling her niece she needed to join the closest Weight Watchers meeting and the next minute she was complimenting her on how great she looked.

"Thanks Auntie. I appreciate it."

Sensing the tension, Kenneth cleared his throat and draped his arms around both of his sisters' shoulders and smiled. "Now, is someone going to help Angelica find that potato salad or are we all going to just suffer without it this year?"

Evelyn's face broke out into a huge grin before they all erupted in laughter.

"Y'all are not right. Junior and Michael love my potato salad. Forget y'all." Angelica said as she laughingly pouted and walked towards the shed where the rest of the family was gathered.

"You know you were wrong for hiding that potato salad," Evelyn said with a raised eyebrow as she laughed and nudged her brother, "but thank goodness you did."

When they were finally alone, Kenneth and Christie slowly walked towards the family. "I'm so glad you could make it, baby girl."

"Me too Daddy."

For Christie, whose parents had divorced when she was young, family had always played a big part in her life. Her father, mother, aunts, uncles and cousins had always been supporting and loving and though they may not have seen each other every day, they were always on each other's minds.

"How's everything going with the new job?"

"It's good. It's keeping me busy and I guess I can't complain about that, right?"

"That's why we paid all that money for school baby girl, so you better not complain."

The scent of barbeque filled Christie's nostrils as she looked at her large family gathered under the roof of the picnic shed. The sounds of the O'Jays blared from the speakers and Christie saw two of her older cousins playing dominos in the corner. Children were running and giggling at nothing in particular while the older women sat around picnic tables and gossiped. Christie felt overwhelmingly full and she hadn't even eaten her first plate of food.

"Chris!" a deep voice yelled from the other end of the shed. She knew from the voice it was Junior, but he looked a whole lot different than she remembered.

The last time she'd seen Junior, which had been almost four years earlier, he had been a little scrawny with a reserved presence. Now, as Christie looked at the 6'2" man barreling toward her, she realized that times had changed.

"Junior? Oh my gosh!" Christie yelled as she ran towards her cousin. It was strange to Christie how she and Junior could go months or years without talking and always pick right back up where they left off.

"Look at you!" Junior said as he embraced her tightly.

"No, look at you!" Christie said as she pulled back from the hug to examine her cousin.

Junior was handsome and there was no getting around it. He also had almond-colored skin, a low haircut, a thin goatee framing his mouth and eyes that pierced you when he smiled.

"Someone's been hitting the gym, huh?" Christie said as she punched the muscles that protruded from his white t-shirt.

Junior smirked and shrugged nonchalantly, "I do what I can."

Kenneth approached them and crossed his arms. "I see the two of you found each other with no problem."

Christie smiled widely and hugged Junior again. "I can't believe it's been four years since I last saw him. Can you believe how big he's gotten, Daddy?" Christie asked as she burrowed her head into her cousin's chest.

"You see how she's talking about me like I'm a puppy dog or something? I'm a grown man, Chris," Junior said as he looked over at Kenneth. "And Uncle Kenneth, I made sure to put the potato salad way in the back of cousin Earl's pick-up truck. Mama will never find it there."

Christie burst out laughing and soon her cousin and father were doing the same.

"I thought you liked your mom's potato salad, Junior. You and Michael are the reason she makes it."

Junior rolled his eyes and shook his head. "Man, I've been scooting that potato salad to the side of the plate for years. I don't like that mess any more than y'all do, but that's my mama so..." he trailed.

"Y'all are a mess," Christie said just as Earl blared into the microphone at the DJ stand.

"Everybody, let's go ahead and pray over the food so we can start eating, okay?"

Had Earl not been her cousin, she would definitely have laughed at the floral shorts and open-toed sandals he sported with his sun hat; but he was family so he got a pass.

"Dear Heavenly Father, we thank you for this time together. We thank you for bringing our Whitfield family home safely so we can rejoice, celebrate, and reignite our love for one another. We're so blessed to have each other and thankful for everything we've been through and will go through, because we know we'll always go through it together. Please bless the food that we are about to receive and the hands that prepared it. In the Lord's name we pray, Amen."

In that moment, Christie looked around at her family and smiled. In the stillness of the after-prayer, she was so overjoyed that she felt like her heart was about to burst. Glancing over at her father and aunts laughing like children, with her cousin and mother standing beside her, Christie knew exactly what it meant to belong. Closing her eyes, Christie took in the moment and said a silent prayer that the feeling inside of her would stay forever; never knowing that life as she knew it was about to change in the blink of an eye.

One

"Let me make you a cup of tea, baby," Anthony said as he eyed Christie's emotionless face.

"I don't want tea," she said blandly.

Anthony turned his attention to the dirty mound of dishes in the kitchen sink. Christie knew she had been inattentive to the things that normally mattered to her, but she couldn't seem to focus. Her home was her castle and usually she was the one to make sure the castle stayed in tip-top shape. On the other hand, Anthony was more laid-back and tried to stay out of his wife's way when it came to cooking and cleaning. Christie had found a balance in her marriage and she liked it. He was the fixer and she was the nurturer. She cooked and kept things tidy, and he fixed whatever was broken.

As Christie lay sprawled on their spacious sectional and glanced up at her husband, she wished he could fix her.

It had been close to a week since her father's death and it was still hard to come to terms with it. Although she wanted to sleep, her mind and her body were in constant competition for her attention and usually her mind won. When Anthony fell asleep at night, she would creep out of bed to curl up on the living room sofa and reminisce about conversations that she'd had with her father; other times she was thinking about the uneasy feeling in her stomach. Although she hadn't accepted her father's death, she wasn't in denial either. Something didn't seem right and it kept her up at night but she couldn't put her finger on what it was.

"Are you hungry? I can heat up some of this lasagna," Anthony asked hoping to snap Christie out of whatever thoughts were swirling around in her head.

Coming out of her daydream, Christie shrugged. Physically, she was hungry—starving even—but emotionally the thought of eating made her sick to her stomach.

"Here let me heat some up. We can eat together, okay?" Anthony said sweetly as he popped the food into the microwave and winked at his wife.

Christie nodded and when Anthony appeared with the food, she moved her legs to make room for him.

"I hope you're hungry because we have Lasagna a' la Anthony," he said jokingly while handing her a plate of mouth-watering lasagna and a slice of garlic bread.

"I always did like your lasagna," Christie said with a smile. Although she wasn't in the mood for talking, she couldn't completely shut out all the things Anthony was doing for her.

"No, you always *loved* my lasagna. Don't act like this lasagna isn't the reason you married me, Chris," Anthony said as he stood up and headed back into the kitchen. "I won't tell anyone you're using me for my cooking skills baby," he called before returning with a bottle of red wine and two glasses.

Christie had a smile on her face and was puzzled that it felt so strange.

"What's wrong?" Anthony asked as he poured the wine and handed Christie her glass.

Christie screwed up her face as she took a swig of the wine. "It just feels… *weird* to smile, to laugh, to live," Christie said. "I kind of feel guilty."

Anthony took a bite of the lasagna and motioned for Christie to finish,

"Guilty about smiling?"

Christie knew she sounded like a rambling fool but she didn't care.

"About living, I guess," she said as she set her glass down and pulled her knees to her chest. "I know my father is gone baby, and there's nothing I can do to bring him back, but I still feel like I shouldn't be smiling and I shouldn't be laughing. I know, I know I sound crazy." Christie stated as she waived her hands around playfully and rolled her eyes.

"No," Anthony said as he held his hand up and slid a little closer to her, "baby, you're supposed to feel *something*. He was your father. You're not crazy because of how you feel."

Christie took a deep breath and bit her bottom lip as she felt a flood of tears coming on. "I'm just realizing I can't pick up the phone and call to ask him how his day is, I can't send him another Father's Day card or surprise him with dinner on the weekend and it hurts," Christie countered as she wiped the tears on her face.

Anthony nodded as he gripped Christie's hand.

"I just want to wake up from this and have it all be some sort of bad dream," Christie said as she tossed her head back and wiped the tears streaming down her cheeks.

As she glanced around the room, she saw two packed suitcases by the front door and dropped her head.

"But then I see those suitcases and I know we're about to get on a plane and head to Chicago so I can bury my father. Then it hits me that there's no waking up from this."

Anthony pulled Christie closer to him and exhaled as she nestled her head into his neck. The two of them sat motionless listening to nothing besides their breathing. As Christie pulled away from Anthony's embrace, she noticed that he had teary eyes as well.

"Let's change the subject," Christie said, forcing a smile.

"No, babe, let's talk. We *need* to talk."

Christie stabbed at the lasagna with her fork and stuffed her mouth.

"How was your day?" she asked, ignoring her husband's request to continue discussing her father's death.

When it came to his wife, Anthony had quickly learned to roll with the punches.

"Well, um, it was interesting. A few of our clients had some glitches with their systems so you know I was running around like crazy. I didn't even eat lunch," Anthony said as he pointed to his food and widened his eyes.

Christie had fallen in love with Anthony's heart more than anything. Yes, he was handsome as all get-out, but the thing she had fallen hard for was his overwhelmingly pure heart. He loved her with everything he had and despite a few glitches early on in their relationship; she did the same with him. They still flirted and amazingly, they still loved each other just as much—if not more than when they first met. Sometimes when she sat in their comfortable suburban home, she wondered how she deserved all the blessings of love and happiness in her life.

Christie peered into her husband's almond-shaped eyes and smiled. Just being around him calmed her down. She watched as he talked intensely with his hands as her smile grew bigger and bigger.

"Hello? Earth to Chris!" Anthony said loudly causing Christie to snap out of her daydream.

"What'd you say?" Christie said picking up her wine glass and taking another sip.

"I asked you about your day."

Her smile quickly disappeared. She had been trying to avoid even thinking about what she had dealt with that day but now that Anthony had brought it up, there was no avoiding it.

"It was horrible, really."

Anthony sat back and rested his plate on his lap, "Why? What happened?"

Christie felt steam rising off her head as she replayed the day's events. It had started as a regular day; Christie was off work and trying to get everything in order for their trip to Chicago for the funeral. Usually on her days off, she thrived on sleeping in, eating horrible food, and watching equally horrible television. That morning though, she had risen at nine and sat at the table all morning with a cup of coffee and the cordless phone.

"Hello, this is Christie Whitfield-Adams. My father, Kenneth Whitfield, is…there. Or his body is," Christie said, slightly flustered.

"Okay," the woman on the other line said shortly.

"I need to speak to someone about his arrangements and make sure everything is taken care of," Christie said quickly. She didn't want to have to be the one to speak *too* much, especially when she hadn't come to terms with Kenneth's death.

"Whitfield, you said?" the woman asked with little emotion.

"Yes ma'am."

"Oh yes, I see here. Well…," she said, her voice trailing off. Christie could tell she was reading something.

"I need to have one of the owners give you a call back. I just answer the phone," she said nonchalantly. "This is really more of their matter."

Christie was confused. "What's more of their matter? I just want to know basic information about my father's services."

She could feel herself getting upset, so she took a few deep breaths and exhaled loudly.

"Ma'am, I can't answer anything because I just transfer calls. If you give me your information, I'll be sure to pass the message along to one of the owners."

Christie rolled her eyes. She wished she was enjoying a trashy episode of Maury.

"And their names are?" Christie asked while grabbing a pen to jot them down.

"Jake and David Thomason."

Christie cradled the phone between her neck and her shoulder and wrote down the information. "Great. Now would you mind transferring me to Deborah? I think she works in the administration office."

"With pleasure," the woman replied before patching her through.

"This is Deborah Matthews, administrative assistant to David Thomason. I'm either on the other line or away from my desk. Please leave a detailed message and I'll return your call as soon as I can."

Christie left a friendly message asking Deborah to call her as soon as she could. She slammed the phone down on the kitchen table and grunted.

When Kenneth and Deborah first started dating, Kenneth initially kept it from Christie. In fact, it wasn't until he was hospitalized that she'd found out they were actually engaged. But Christie had always known her father to be very selective and private about the women he brought around her, even as an adult. So when Kenneth passed away it was decided that his body would be sent to the Thomason Funeral Home where Deborah worked part-time. Christie was sure her father would get the royal treatment.

It had been almost a full day since she had first tried to make contact with the funeral home and Deborah; Christie was starting to get a little uneasy. She tried phoning her aunts to see if they had any insight, but like Deborah and the funeral home, everyone was giving her the runaround. Christie was through playing nice with them. She wanted answers and she was going to get them.

Reaching for the obituary section of the newspaper, Christie scanned the names until she found what she was looking for and picked up the phone.

"Hello, my name is Mildred Fox. I would like to speak to the owner regarding Theodore Fox. He's my father."

"Sure thing," the receptionist said and quickly transferred "Mildred" through to someone. Christie was shocked at how easily she was connected by simply using a person's name from the paper. Her investigative skills were still intact.

"This is Jake, how can I help you?"

Christie was livid. Why was it so easy to get the owner on the phone when she posed at someone else but virtually impossible to get them on the phone for herself?

"Yes, this is Christie Whitfield-Adams. My father, Kenneth Whitfield, is there in your funeral home."

Christie could hear the man scrambling and trying to figure out a response.

"I've been trying to get either you or your brother on the phone for an entire day."

"Mrs. Adams, yes uh…I'm sorry about that. I was actually out of the country and just returned today. My brother was handling everything with your father so let me see if I can locate any files. Was there anything in particular you wanted assistance with?"

"I just want to know what's going on, that's all."

Christie was already fed up. Something was going on, and the way he was acting told her that she was right on the money with her suspicions.

Jake shuffled through what seemed like mounds of paper and Christie heard him moving around the office. She knew she had caught him off guard, but she didn't care.

"Mrs. Adams, I hate to do this to you but can I have my brother give you a call in about half an hour? He has handled your father personally and I'd much rather he spoke to you and gave you accurate information."

Christie rolled her eyes and imagined the fear on his face when he realized he wasn't talking to "Mildred Fox" but instead to a crafty Christie Whitfield-Adams.

"Fine, you said he'll call in thirty minutes?" Christie asked defiantly.

"Yes. Yes ma'am, he will," Jake said with relief.

"Great. And can you tell me if Deborah is in today or is she still away from her desk?"

Christie could hear Jake smiling through the phone. Probably relieved the pressure was off him, as he answered, "Yes, she's in. I actually just saw her sitting at her desk. Would you like me to transfer you?"

Christie cut her eyes and shook her head. That alarming feeling in her stomach was coming back. "No, that's okay. I look forward to speaking with your brother in thirty minutes," Christie said before she hung up.

She took a sip of her now cold coffee, poured another cup, grabbed the cordless phone, and settled at the kitchen table. There was no way she was going to miss this call.

"And what happened?" Anthony asked as he leaned forward and prepared for Christie to finish the story.

Christie closed her eyes and pointed to the kitchen counter.

"You see that cup of coffee sitting on the counter? It's the *same* cup of coffee I poured in anticipation of my conversation with Mr. Thomason."

Anthony's eyes widened. "He never called?"

"He never called," Christie exhaled and said. "Something's going on Anthony. I can feel it in my heart. I've tried calling Deborah and no one at the funeral home will even call me back."

Anthony was usually the skeptic in their relationship, the one who thought everything was a conspiracy theory; nevertheless, this time, he had a feeling Christie was really on to something.

"Well, maybe when we get to Chicago we can go straight to the funeral home," Anthony said just as the phone rang.

"Hello? Yes, she sure is, hold on," Anthony said as he passed the phone to Christie.

"It's your mom. I'm going to change out of my work clothes. I'll be back," Anthony said retreating to the bedroom.

"Hey, Ma," Christie said extending her legs and stretching.

"Hey baby girl. How was your day?"

Christie didn't have the heart to tell the same story all over again, but she did.

"Well, baby, the only thing to do is to wait until you get here so we can see what's really going on. I started to call Angelica today but...you know."

Christie did know. Like her daughter, Alise just wanted to wake up from this bad dream. Christie's heart ached heavily for what she imagined her mother must be going through. Although they hadn't been married for years, her parents still loved each other.

"What time do you land?" Alise asked, breaking the silence.

"I don't even know. I think our plane leaves at eight in the morning. Anthony knows."

"How is my son-in-law?"

Christie smiled. Her mother had always loved Anthony, and for that Christie was glad.

"He's fine. He's upstairs getting undressed."

"So, about those grandbabies," Alise said with a chuckle.

"Maaaa…"

The two of them laughed in an attempt to ease their pain.

"Your father always wanted grandchildren. It was all he talked about when you were in college."

"Really?" Christie asked with surprise.

"Oh yeah. He couldn't wait to spoil your children rotten. I think a part of him just wanted to make your children unbearable for you," Alise laughed softly. "He was always so funny about it, too."

Christie tried to smile but a part of her felt like hanging up right then and there.

"Ma, I really need to get some rest. I'll call you when we're about to board the plane."

"Okay, baby. Remember, stop thinking so much and start relaxing a bit. This weekend is going to be long and hard for both of us."

Christie dropped her head.

"But, hey, this is a celebration of life. You know your father would not have wanted you to be all sad about anything. He was *full* of life, Christie," Alise said as her voice cracked.

"I know Ma. I know."

Still, her heart ached for what she knew and ultimately, for what she *didn't* know.

Two

"You'll be boarding at gate C22," the skycap said as he handed Christie two tickets. He was an older man who reminded her of her grandfather. He had chocolate skin with salt and pepper scattered throughout his thinning hair. While Christie watched him toss their bags onto the conveyer belt, she reached into her pocket, pulled four dollars out and handed it to him.

"Here you go. Thank you," Christie replied sweetly.

"Why thank you, baby girl," the man said as he took the money and tipped his cap downwards.

Hearing the words "baby girl" almost made Christie break down but she held it together and forced a smile. Here she was heading to Chicago to bury her father and countless forced smiles could not erase the sadness surrounding her.

"That was nice," Anthony said as they headed toward the line of people waiting to have their bags checked.

"What do you mean?" Christie asked as she shifted her laptop bag from one side to the other.

"I've never really seen you tip a skycap before. Heck, I don't even think I've ever seen you tip *anyone* before," Anthony joked as he slowed his pace and looked down at his wife.

Christie shrugged. "It was nothing. He just looked like he deserved it."

But it *was* something and Christie knew it. For as long as she could remember, her father had always been the big tipper in their family. He generously tipped waiters, skycaps and valets. Christie had asked him over and over why he tipped so much and he always told her it would make sense when she got older.

"When you get older, you'll be more appreciative of people who give great service," Kenneth said one evening over spaghetti and meatballs as a fourteen year old Christie sat Indian-style listening to her father.

"A dollar or two is fine, Daddy, but you like to tip five, ten, fifteen and twenty dollars!"

Kenneth slurped up a noodle and winked at his child. "You'll understand when you're older, baby girl."

"Christie, you're next," Anthony said nudging his wife to the podium where the TSA worker checked boarding passes and IDs.

Her mind should have been focused on getting to their gate, but it was everywhere else.

"Thanks," the overweight TSA worker said after checking her identification and returning her boarding pass. Christie promptly moved forward and began the draining process of stripping off her jacket, shoes and jewelry while taking her laptop out of its case.

"This is why I hate traveling," Christie mumbled as she went through the metal detector and then headed to collect her things. After gathering everything, she turned and waited for Anthony to do the same.

"What gate are we at again?" Christie asked.

"C22," Anthony replied as he quickened his pace to match hers.

"C…22?" Christie repeated as she felt her chest tightening.

She had been to that airport many times, flying all over the country, but her mind stuck on the first time she'd traveled to Chicago after learning of her father's hospitalization.

It was a chilly day in February when she'd made the exact same trek of checking her boarding pass to scrambling to find her gate. She had been running a few minutes late and wanted to be certain she made it to her gate on time.

Come on, come on, Christie remembered saying to herself as she started practically jogging.

The call she had received from her mother the day before telling her that her father been admitted to the hospital was indelibly etched in her brain. Her mother urged her not to worry but knew that she would. Christie booked a flight to Chicago for the next morning to see for herself what was going on with her father.

Stopping in her tracks, Christie had looked at her boarding pass and scrunched up her face.

"Do you need some help, darling?" an older woman asked as she slowed down and cocked her head to the side. Christie assumed she worked at the airport by the uniform she was wearing.

"I'm looking for...for..." Christie stumbled as she pulled out her boarding pass, "Gate C22."

"It's right this way," the woman said pointing toward a line of people waiting to board the plane.

"Thank you. Thank you so much," Christie said as she jogged over to the line.

The flight was uneventful but allowed Christie the opportunity to catch up on her reading. She was nervous, even if she couldn't fully admit it, but hoped reading would take her mind off her worries.

She wasn't sure what to expect. For as long as Christie could remember, she had never seen her father with more than an occasional bronchitis flare up and now he was lying in a hospital bed. She tried not to think about it, but she knew it had to be serious for him to be admitted.

After she got off the plane and headed to the baggage claim Christie called Anthony, "Hey babe. I landed."

"Are you a little calmer now?" Anthony asked sweetly. He had been just as worried about Christie as he was about Kenneth. Although she thought she handled it perfectly, Christie rarely handled stress well.

"I'm as calm as I can be, I guess," Christie said as she took a deep breath and before barreling through the crowd of people. "I just hope Evelyn is on time to pick me up."

Anthony snickered, "I can't believe Evelyn, of all people, is the one who volunteered to pick you up."

Christie rolled her eyes and sighed. She definitely would have preferred her Aunt Angelica to pick her up, but she understood Evelyn was the only one available.

"Let's hope neither she nor I end up in the hospital, too," Christie joked.

"Behave, baby," Anthony replied through his laughs.

Anthony was her source of normalcy and peace and she hated that he was unable to accompany her on the trip to check on her father.

"You know I wish I could be there with you, right?" Anthony said just as she finished her thought.

"Yeah, baby, I know. You're busy right now at work. I understand," she said as she tried to force herself to be okay with handling everything on her own.

"Everything will be fine, remember that. Through it all, everything will be fine."

Christie nodded just as she saw her bag coming around the conveyer belt.

"Baby, I see my bag. I'll call you once I get to the hospital. I love you." Christie said as Anthony repeated the same three words.

As Christie lugged her bag outside to the pick-up area, she immediately spotted her Aunt Evelyn's black Chevy Tahoe and headed towards it.

"You got it?" Evelyn asked as she rolled down the window.

"Yeah, I've got it," Christie said through gritted teeth as she rolled her eyes at her aunt's behavior. It had been months since she'd seen her aunt and she didn't even have the decency to get out and hug her own niece.

After throwing her bag into the car, Christie hopped in the passenger seat and fastened her seatbelt. Her aunt looked over with a strange smirk on her face.

"Was your flight alright?" Evelyn asked as she put the car in drive and sped off into traffic.

"It was fine," Christie replied as she checked her phone for nothing in particular.

"Your daddy has been asking about you non-stop since he talked to you yesterday. You know you didn't have to come up, right? Everything's okay."

Christie nodded, "I know, but he's my father. I just wanted to check for myself. No offense, of course."

"None taken."

The two rode in silence for what seemed like an eternity before they both found themselves humming to the same Beyoncé song on the radio.

"You like Beyoncé, Aunt Evelyn?" Christie said as she sat back in the leather seat and crossed her arms. Finally, something they had in common.

"She's okay. I think I like her music more than I like her," Evelyn said with a chuckle.

Christie smirked and stared out of the window before clearing her throat.

"So how's dad been doing?" Christie asked, changing the subject.

Evelyn shrugged, put on her signal, and then turned into the parking lot of the hospital.

"He's been okay. It was scary at first," Evelyn said while maneuvering the car into the narrow space.

Christie had not heard the entire story of what exactly had happened with her father. All she knew was that her mother said he had been hospitalized.

"What happened, Aunt Evelyn?"

Evelyn took a deep breath, laid her head back on the headrest and started talking.

"Deborah found him," she said lifting her head slightly off the headrest. Christie had never even heard the name before and now she was being told a stranger, a woman named Deborah, had found her father?

"Who's Deborah?" Christie frowned and asked.

"Your father's girlfriend…fiancée…whatever," Evelyn said before dropping her head back on the headrest.

Christie exhaled and looked out of the window at a couple holding hands. Nothing was making sense. Still, she asked Evelyn to continue.

"Deborah told the 911 operator that she had been talking to your father earlier in the day and he didn't sound too good. She said the last time they spoke he sounded weak and she told him to leave the front door unlocked so she could check on him. When she got there he was unconscious."

Christie felt a piece of her heart drop. She knew her father was mortal, but to hear it vocalized stung a bit. It was like the moments when she realized Santa Claus and Superman were make-believe.

"Deborah followed the ambulance and said by the time they arrived at the hospital, they'd resuscitated Kenneth. Deborah was the one who called to tell me your dad was in the hospital. She used the emergency contact list to find me."

As Christie struggled to take it all in, more questions surfaced.

"And this Deborah woman…what do we know about her?"

Evelyn rolled her eyes and smacked her teeth at the same time, "I don't trust her, simple as that."

Christie peered over at her aunt who was talking with her eyes closed and for the first time she witnessed her aunt's vulnerability; a big sister trying to come to grips with her younger brother's illness. For once in her life, Evelyn couldn't bully herself into control and Christie could see how she was struggling with that. She had always been there to protect him. Kenneth, Evelyn and Angelica were the three who always had each other's backs. Now, as Kenneth lay in the hospital, Christie wondered how two of the closest people in his life were handling it.

"But your father…well, your father seems to like her enough to call her his girlfriend, or fiancée, whatever."

"Dad is getting remarried after all these years?" Christie asked with a chuckle.

"Right. I told him he was going to have to lose a few pounds before he put on a tuxedo. And they'll probably have to marry in the summer or fall because his bronchitis is always acting up this time of year."

Christie couldn't handle even thinking about her father remarrying right then, but knew her aunt was talking out of anxiety. Then the light bulb went off in Christie's head.

"It's probably his bronchitis, right? I mean, he does always have really bad episodes in colder weather. Maybe the doctor just needs to give him a stronger prescription or something," Christie said as she looked over to her aunt for reassurance.

"I sure hope so, Chris," she replied, not hiding her nervousness.

"Well, let me get on up there and check on him. You coming up?" Christie asked as she grabbed her purse and reached for the door.

"Yeah, I'm coming. Just give me a few minutes. I need to call my salon and make sure everything's okay, I just hired someone to manage the salon in my absence since I have been out here at the hospital every day," Evelyn said.

Christie made her way up to room 643, pushed the heavy door open and saw her father lying in the bed watching television. He didn't realize she had entered the room until he heard her sneakers squeaking on the floor.

"Baby girl," her father said as he lifted his head and smiled weakly.

"Hey, Daddy," Christie replied as she set her purse down on the chair and walked towards him.

There were so many machines and beeping sounds going on that Christie almost felt afraid to touch her own father. But as she got closer and saw his familiar grin, she broke out of that fear and leaned down to hug and kiss him.

"How are you feeling, old man?" she joked as she took a seat on the edge of the bed.

"I've felt better, baby girl, but I think I'm improving," Kenneth sighed as he tried to sit up.

"No, just lay there, Daddy," Christie smiled as she patted his hand.

"How'd you get here?" he asked sitting up anyway.

Christie shook her head at her stubborn father, "Evelyn picked me up from the airport. She's coming up in a few minutes."

Kenneth smiled and nodded his head.

"What happened, Daddy?" Christie blurted out.

Shrugging his shoulders, Kenneth let out a loud exhale. "I wish I knew. One moment I was feeling okay and then I wasn't. The next thing I remember was waking up in the hospital. Thank God Deborah came over."

Christie didn't want to harp too much on the illness keeping her father in the hospital, so she switched subjects.

"So, tell me about this Deborah person. You're getting a goofy little grin when you say her name," Christie joked as she nudged her father.

Kenneth shook his head and smiled. "Deborah and I have known each other for almost six years now. We bumped into each other about a year ago and started dating. She's great, Chris. You'll like her," Kenneth said proudly.

Christie only really knew about the serious relationships in her father's life. There had been Pam, who had been nice but too controlling, and Tina who loved Kenneth much more than he loved her. Thinking back, those two were the only women he had ever introduced to his daughter.

"So...you're engaged, Daddy? I'd better meet this fiancée Deborah...," Christie trailed as the hospital door opened.

"I hear my name and I hope it's all good things," a woman said as she sashayed into the room with a bag in her hand.

"You must be Christie. I've heard so much about you and seen so many pictures. I'm Deborah," she finished as she sat the bag down in a chair next to Christie's bag, and extended her hand.

Christie smiled and took in the woman's appearance. She was pretty, far prettier than Christie had expected, and she was tiny; a size six to be exact. Deborah was light-skinned with dark shoulder-length hair that was curled under slightly. Christie could tell she was in her fifties simply by her demeanor, but she didn't look a day over forty-five.

"Hi! It's so nice to finally meet you," Christie said as she gripped the woman's hand and smiled.

"I was just bringing your dad some good old fried chicken from KFC. He loves KFC chicken," Deborah said with a wink.

Christie stepped back from the bed and allowed Deborah to set the food up on the hospital tray for her father. Smells of chicken, mashed potatoes and biscuits filled the air. Christie wasn't sure whether her father was supposed to have KFC, but she wasn't about to say anything.

"Baby girl, I need you to do me a favor," Kenneth said as he stuffed a piece of chicken in his mouth. "Here's my bank information. I need you to make a run to the bank and withdraw this much money," he said as he pointed at an amount written on a piece of paper he handed to her.

"I need to pay my bills and I really wasn't expecting to be cooped up in the hospital."

"Well, maybe someone just needed to slow down a little bit," Deborah said as she stroked his arm softly.

Christie took her purse and the bank information and leaned over to kiss her father on the cheek.

"Okay, Daddy. It's still the same bank on Central Avenue?" she inquired.

Her father nodded and took a swig of water.

"Hey, hey," Evelyn said as she entered the room, "it smells good in here."

"Have some chicken," Deborah said pointing to the open box on the counter.

"I'm okay," Evelyn replied as she took a seat and focused her attention on the television, "Are you feeling okay, brother?"

"I feel better now that three of my favorite women are here," Kenneth announced.

"Aunt Evelyn, do you mind driving me to the bank?"

Evelyn looked at Kenneth and then back at Christie before tossing her the keys, "Drive yourself."

Christie rolled her eyes and headed out. She had driven the route to her father's bank many times, usually to withdraw money from the ATM, so it wasn't hard.

Inside the bank, Christie slid her father's note to the teller saying, "Hi, my name is Christie Whitfield-Adams and my father, Kenneth Adams, banks here. He was hospitalized yesterday and sent me over to withdraw some money for his bills. Is there any other information you need?"

The teller punched in a few numbers then called over her manager. The manager, an overweight white man with a horrible comb over and thick trifocal glasses asked Christie to step into his office.

"I hope your father starts feeling better," he said as he closed the office door.

"Thanks," Christie replied in confusion. Why was she in his office?

"Christie, your father does not have you listed as holding his Power of Attorney or POA so, unfortunately, we cannot release any funds to you," he said.

"Okay, so what do we do? His bills have to get paid," Christie asked curiously.

The manager reached into his desk, pulled out a few documents and slid them towards Christie.

"It's pretty simple. You'll need your father to fill these out naming you as his POA, sign them and have them notarized. Once we get them back, you'll be able to access his account at any time."

Christie gathered the papers and made her way back to the hospital.

"Hey baby girl, you didn't spend all my money in one place did you?" Kenneth asked playfully.

"They wouldn't let me take anything out because I'm not listed as a Power of Attorney for your accounts."

Kenneth sucked his teeth. "Man, I totally forgot about that. Okay, well, Evelyn and Angelica are both already listed as my POAs. Do you want me to change it so you are instead?"

Christie thought about it for a moment. On one hand, she thought it was the responsible thing to do; on the other hand, she knew logistically it didn't make any sense. Aunt Evelyn and Aunt Angelica lived in the same city as her father and could readily access his financial information, if needed. Christie glanced over at Evelyn, who was trying to act like she wasn't listening.

"Daddy, it makes more sense for Evelyn and Angelica to be the POAs. You know, in case anything happens and I'm all the way in Indianapolis," Christie said.

Kenneth nodded and winked at his daughter, "You're always thinking things through, baby girl, just like I taught you."

Christie smiled at the thought of making her father proud and took a seat. She listened and watched as Evelyn, Kenneth and Deborah interacted and somewhere deep down inside, she wanted to believe this was the start of something great. Her Aunt Evelyn was acting nicer and her father seemed to be genuinely happy with Deborah.

"Chris," Anthony called out, snapping his wife from her daydream, "give me your carry-on so I can store it in the bin."

Christie hadn't even realized she'd boarded the plane. As she took her window seat, she rested her forehead against the cold plastic and exhaled. The idea of "something great" just a few months earlier in a crowded hospital room filled with smells of chicken and biscuits had ended up being the end of something greater.

Three

"Can you pass me that box, honey?" Christie asked softly as she gazed around the home that had once been filled with laughter and her father's scent. Now, as she sniffed the air, she wondered if she would ever be able to experience that smell and familiarity again.

Christie leaned her head against the wall in the living room and took a deep breath. No one could have prepared her for the fact that she was going to have to bury the person she considered her superhero so unexpectedly.

Glancing around her father's home, she smiled. Almost every inch had a memory attached to it. He had been a hardworking man and the two-bedroom apartment he had called home when she was a child was now a six-bedroom house with the finest furnishings. To put it plainly, Kenneth was wealthy beyond words. Everything about her father had been an inspiration, from his humble beginnings to putting himself and then Christie through school, to owning properties throughout Chicago. Christie was proud to have had Kenneth as her father and more importantly, she was proud to have learned from him.

"This one?" Anthony asked as he approached his wife with a mid-sized box.

Christie nodded and seated herself on a loveseat. Anthony took the cue and sat beside her. Throughout their relationship, Anthony had always served as her rock. When she was working late nights and needed food or encouragement, Anthony had never missed being there for her. When she was going through any situation, Anthony was there.

"Are you sure you're okay with looking through this, babe?" Anthony asked as he rubbed her back. Anthony knew how close Christie and her father had been and he never told Christie, but losing Kenneth was almost like losing his own father. When he started dating Christie, the two of them immediately clicked and when they married, he felt he inherited the father he'd never had.

"I'm sure. I have to do this sooner or later, right?" she asked without wanting a reply, as she lifted the top off the box.

Christie moved in silence but her mind was racing a mile a minute. She wanted to take everything in and feel connected to her father in some way, shape or form. In the box lay hundreds of pictures. Sure, they were pictures Christie had seen before, but now Christie allowed her fingers to caress the time worn photo where her father stood—strong, smiling and happy. She wanted to teleport back in time and experience her dad in *this* element; she wanted to erase the last few months of his illness.

"Wow, Kenneth looks so young there," Anthony said as he smiled at the picture of his father-in-law posing in a sharp suit with his arm draped over the shoulders of an unidentified female. He looked young then and Christie thought the picture was probably taken years before he and her mother crossed paths. In the picture her father was smiling widely, a thick beard covered his almond face and his white teeth. He was wearing dark shades and his hair was lined perfectly. Before she knew it, Christie felt herself smiling so hard her cheeks began to hurt.

"He *was* happy. He was *always* happy," Anthony said as he stroked Christie's free hand.

She looked up at her husband as reality set in. Hearing "was" always shocked her back into reality. He was gone. No matter how many times she told herself he was just around the corner, he was gone.

"He was healthy as ever as far as I knew, honey. How did this happen to him, of all people?" Christie asked, closing her eyes. She didn't want an explanation. All she wanted was someone to tell her it had all been a mistake. She had often wondered how she would feel when she lost one of her parents, but now at just thirty-one years old, she had no idea it would come *this* soon.

"I wish I knew, Chris." Anthony replied. He was also suffering and wanted answers too.

Sensing the need to change the subject, Anthony picked an over-sized picture from beneath the pile and chuckled. "Hey, hey, look at Pops."

"Daddy with Mayor Piedmont," Christie said proudly. "I remember when he took that picture."

Christie remembered almost every conversation she'd ever had with her father including the night he'd met and taken a picture with the mayor.

"*Chris, your dad is a celebrity—well, kind of,*" Kenneth had told her over the phone as she was studying in her dorm room.

"*A celebrity, Daddy? I have to hear more.*"

"*Well, tonight at our annual university banquet, the Mayor surprised me with a special presentation for all of the accomplishments your father has achieved since being president of the school,*" Kenneth said proudly.

Christie remembered grinning as widely as if she'd been honored herself.

"*The Mayor presented me with a plaque, a gift certificate and Bulls tickets!*" The small things excited her father and she loved him for that.

"*Daddy, I'm so proud of you. Did you get pictures?*" Christie asked.

"*Of course. I'll have to send you one. I'm framing this one and hanging it in my house,*" Kenneth said with a goofy laugh.

Even in the silliest of moments, though, he always found a way to bring it back to a life lesson. "*This is why it's important to stay true to what you believe in, baby girl. A lot of the things I tried to do at the university, people told me were foolish to even think of taking on; but I did it anyway. Sometimes you have to step out on what you know is right and disregard what everyone else thinks is right. Life isn't about making every right decision and opening every right door, baby girl; it's about building up the courage and strength to turn the knob.*"

Christie always found it funny that her father could go from comedian to professor in two seconds flat. Still, she was grateful for him and his guidance. It was because of him that Christie had pressed on in college, though she had often toyed with the idea of dropping out. Kenneth had given Christie everything she needed to succeed so she wasn't about to let him down.

"He looks so proud in this picture—like he won a million dollars," Anthony said.

"He won the respect of his peers that night. I remember it like it was yesterday. It feels like it was yesterday, too."

Christie took one last look at the picture and stood up. Her heels clicked against the tile as she headed to the kitchen. Christie reached for a glass from the cabinet and filled it with filtered water from the sink. Her mouth suddenly became dry.

"You okay?" Anthony asked as he walked into the kitchen and leaned against the counter. He knew his wife well enough to know the answer, but still he asked.

"I just got hot for no reason. I feel lightheaded, too. There's just so much going on right now, honey. I want to be strong because I know that's what he'd want me to do, but being strong makes me feel so weak to my own emotions," she said as she allowed her eyes to fill with tears.

Anthony cradled Christie in his arms and rocked until her whimpering ceased.

"This isn't going away overnight, Chris. You're going to need to heal and even then you'll never fully get over him being gone. But I'm here."

Christie wasn't sure what she'd done to luck up on such a dynamic husband but she was thankful. Anthony was tall, strong-minded, loving and most of all, he put up with all her quirks. The fact that he was so handsome and made other women swoon was icing on the cake for Christie.

"Thank you, baby," she said as she leaned forward and placed her lips upon his. This was the one place that still felt familiar. When they broke from their embrace, Christie continued looking around the kitchen while sipping her water.

"What do you think you're going to do with your dad's house?"

Christie shrugged, "I don't know. It's too far for us to live here but maybe we can rent it out. Daddy had this house paid off ten years ago so there's no mortgage payment."

Anthony nodded. Part of him felt strange about making plans for Kenneth's belongings and home, but the other part of him knew it was necessary.

"And what about his rental properties and cars? Did you have a chance to call the bank?"

Christie smiled to herself. Her husband rambled when he was nervous and as upset as she was; she knew he was emotional as well.

"That reminds me," she said as she put the glass down on the marble countertop, "I should call the bank now. I had them freeze the accounts the day Daddy died, but I need to make sure they don't want any additional information from me."

Punching in the numbers on her cell phone, Christie laid her head on Anthony's shoulder as the line rang.

"Hi, this is Christie Whitfield-Adams. My father, Kenneth Whitfield, was a customer of your bank and he passed away recently. I had his accounts frozen but wanted to see if there was anything else you needed from me."

Christie listened intensely as the woman on the other line spoke quickly and firmly.

"Yes, uh huh. Yes ma'am. That's correct," she said pulling away from Anthony and moving to the other side of the room.

Something was happening. Something wasn't right.

"Ma'am. Wait, repeat that for me," she said as she put her cell on speakerphone. She wanted to make sure she wasn't hearing what she thought she was hearing.

"My name is Sara Frederick. I'm one of the managers of the bank," the woman said. "Can you hear me?"

She sounded like she couldn't have been more than twenty-five years old and a chipper, blonde-haired, blue-eyed woman of German American decent. Her tone was helpful but Christie could sense the nervousness in her voice.

"I can hear you. Please repeat what you said," Christie said quickly.

"At the time you froze your father's account, there was $1,100 in it."

"That has to be a mistake, ma'am. My father had *way* more money than $1,100 and he's been banking with you all since I was a child. Please check it again." Christie said as Anthony looked at her suspiciously.

"Mrs. Adams, I've checked it a few times. I knew your father. He was a nice man, but this is what was in his account at the time you called to freeze everything."

Christie dropped her cell phone on the tile floor and screamed. She thought something hadn't been right; she had felt it in her veins. Now she knew.

"Do you hear this, Anthony? Do you?" Christie yelled, her voice echoing throughout the house.

"Babe, calm down until we can find out what's going on. We'll go up to the bank first thing in the morning and figure this out."

Christie stared at her shaking hands as she stepped over her cracked cell phone and headed to the house phone cradled against the wall.

"No, we're going to figure this out now," she said as she angrily dialed a familiar number.

"Hello?" Angelica said sweetly into the phone.

"Aunt Angel, this is Christie."

"Hey, Chris. How are you holding up, honey?" Aunt Angelica asked in a so-sweet-it-must-be-fake tone.

"I could actually be doing better. I just got off the phone with the bank and they told me that my father's account only had $1,100 in it at the time of his death. Do you know anything about this?" she asked, placing her free hand on her hip.

There were a few moments of silence before Angelica answered.

"Sweetheart, I have no idea about your father's finances. Are they sure that's all he had in there?" she asked, trying to force concern in her voice.

"Positive." Christie said shortly. She wasn't buying her aunt's act at all; not this time.

"That's strange, darling. Maybe we can talk about it later," she said, trying to brush off Christie.

Without even saying goodbye, Christie hung up the phone and dialed her Aunt Evelyn's number. She had so much rage running through her veins; she prayed she wouldn't say anything *too* foul to her least-favorite aunt.

"Hello?" Evelyn said, clearing her throat.

"Aunt Ev, this is Christie."

"Yeah, okay?"

Christie should have known right then the conversation wasn't going to end well but she wanted to get to the bottom of things.

"I just spoke to the bank and they told me my father only had $1,100 in his account at the time of his death. Do you know anything about this?"

Immediately Evelyn started throwing heat back.

"Why are you calling *me* with this? Aren't *you* his next of kin? Shouldn't *you* have been on top of this?"

"Wait, are you serious right now, Aunt Evelyn? I'm calling to ask you what's going on with my father's account, because everyone knows you and Aunt Angelica were his Power of Attorneys, and you're putting this back on me?"

By this time, they were screaming at each other.

"Listen, child, don't call my phone with any accusations or insinuations until you have proof. Your father wasn't the best with managing his money. Who knows where it went!"

Christie couldn't believe her ears. Her aunts, the ones who worshipped the ground their baby brother—her father—walked on, were now acting as though he was a stranger. Christie's heart started to hurt. It was pain she had never felt before.

"All I want to know is what is going on, that's all," Christie screamed back. "The two of you were here and my father trusted you. If you did anything to—"

Before she could finish her sentence, Evelyn hung up on her.

Christie's repeated attempts at calling both sisters back, were met with only busy signals and voicemails.

"I don't believe this," Christie said as she slid down the wall of the foyer.

Anthony stood silent beside her, equally confused and angry, and shook his head.

"This *can't* be my family," Christie said as she looked up to Anthony with tears streaming down her face. "This *can't* be my family."

Anthony was at a loss for words. He wanted to be enraged too but he was just flabbergasted.

In a split second, Christie was standing up searching the room.

"Anthony, I'm heading over to Aunt Angelica's and Uncle Michael's house. I've got to sort this out and I've got to sort it out now," she said as she found her purse.

"Baby, just wait a second."

"I must be in the twilight zone, right? This can't *really* be happening. Look, don't worry about coming with me. This is my family and if anything happens to go down, I don't want you to be involved in it at all. If I need you, I'll call."

"Wait, I'll go wi—," Anthony finally sputtered as Christie slammed the front door.

He watched in dismay as his frantic and anxious wife sped out of the driveway.

Four

Christie couldn't believe her ears.

"What do you mean she wants me to leave?" she asked so loudly she startled herself.

She glanced around the few people standing at the entrance of her Aunt Angelica's home and squinted. Everyone looked as if they knew what was going on but unfortunately, they weren't sharing anything with her.

Crossing her arms, Christie raised her eyebrows as high as they could go while looking around for someone, anyone, to talk. After a brief moment of silence, Christie shrugged her shoulders and started walking towards the front door of her aunt's home. She saw Angelica's husband Michael walking towards her and slowed her pace.

"Christie, you need to leave," he said with certainty in his voice.

Christie took a deep breath and placed her hands on top of her head. She wanted to make sense out of everything that was happening but she couldn't.

"You have got to be kidding me!" Christie said as she paced back and forth. She could see everyone was staring at her as if she had seven heads and two mouths, but she didn't care.

"Look," she warned Michael in a serious tone, "if she thinks for one minute that I'm about to let her get away with this crap, then she's sadly mistaken."

"Christie, I don't know what's going on between you and your aunt, but this is neither the place nor the time. You need to show some respect and leave our home," Michael said with an equally serious tone. In all the years she'd known him, Christie had never seen Michael this aggressive, especially not with her. She'd had enough of him.

"Did you just use the word respect? You, of all people?" shouted Christie as she took two steps towards him.

She wasn't sure if he was afraid of her coming towards him with all her anger and hostility or if he felt sorry for her. Either way, Christie didn't care. She had put up with a lot from her family over the past few weeks and the last thing she needed now was additional stress.

"Don't make me laugh," she continued, "you don't know the meaning of respect."

Christie could feel beads of sweat building above her top lip- a trait she'd inherited from her father that always signaled stress- instinctively she wiped away the moisture. She had every reason to feel stressed, not only was her father gone, but it felt like every part of her life she regarded as being normal was slowly disappearing too.

"It's clear you missed that lesson yourself," Michael retorted as he looked her up and down for longer than was acceptable. There was something in his eyes and voice that made Christie cringe. She didn't like the tone he was taking with her, when all she wanted was answers.

"Bastard!" she shouted as his eyes lingered on her hips.

Christie kept her eyes locked on Michael's and took a deep breath. She could feel her chest rising and falling as she breathed through her nose. Even with all of her anger, nothing could have prepared Christie for what came out of his mouth.

"Chris, I can see that you're upset but I need you to leave. You are not welcome here. Now if you can't seem to understand that, maybe the police can help clear things up for you."

It was as if Christie was hearing him in slow motion or in another language. She shook her head from side to side to be sure she'd heard exactly what she thought she was hearing. Her uncle—the husband of her father's sister—couldn't be threatening to call the police on her, right? In a flash, Christie thought back to the time she had so often spent with her family at reunions, barbecues or celebratory events and her eyes filled with angry tears. What had come over her family?

"Are you threatening me?" Christie questioned with her eyebrows raised. By now, her face was hot and her sweaty upper lip was back with a vengeance.

"Is that what you're telling me, Michael? You're calling the cops on me? Go right ahead, what are you going to tell them? The daughter of your deceased brother-in-law has questions and no one is willing to answer them so they should arrest me?" she rambled, everything on her mind was coming out of her mouth at a rapid pace.

"I think it's best that you leave," Michael stated with finality.

Christie could tell she wasn't getting anywhere with Michael. Even though he wasn't the one with the answers she needed, she still wanted the respect due to her. Unsure of whether to punch the so-called man standing in front of her or to just leave, Christie stood firm and crossed her arms across her chest while she took in her surroundings. This was the house where she had spent so many evenings as a child—the same house she had trick-or-treated while growing up and in fact, the house she had often stayed in while visiting her dying father in the hospital. Now the house looked different. She could see her aunt in the huge bay window that overlooked the front lawn with a phone pressed to her ear. Christie couldn't believe everything that was happening. She had only come over for answers and now she was being threatened with being arrested.

By this time, several neighbors had come out of their palatial homes to stand on their immaculate lawns and get a peek at all of the yelling. Christie knew without a doubt this would tear her aunt up more than anything. As big as her Aunt Angelica had always been on perception and perfection, Christie was sure she hated that the neighbors would see cracks in her perfect life. On the inside, Christie was overjoyed that her aunt was being exposed, though on the outside she was fuming.

"Look, Michael, you can ask my aunt to either come down here and give me the answers I need or she can just deal with her wonderful neighbors watching all of this unfold," Christie said with defiance.

Michael looked back up at the window and took a deep breath while Angelica talked angrily into the phone. Christie could tell she was yelling by the way that the veins in her neck bulged.

Christie paced up and down the driveway, waiting for Michael or Angelica to give her what she wanted, when she overheard two of the neighbors whispering.

"Is that Christie Whitfield-Adams, the reporter?" she heard a white-haired, pale-skinned woman ask her friend, who looked almost identical to her. If Christie hadn't been watching it unfold before her, she might have thought they were extras on the television show *The Golden Girls*.

It had been years since she started her career as a weekend reporter for a local television station in Chicago. When she relocated to Indianapolis and accepted a position at KTL as a reporter, she settled into the idea of always being a "familiar face" to people. After leaving KTL and accepting a position as a Public Relations Manager for a popular radio station, Christie thought she'd freed herself from the stares of fans that watched her every move. Seeing her aunt's neighbors, though, she knew she was wrong.

Everything was happening so fast, Christie thought as she fought back the tears. Under normal circumstances, she would never let anyone see her sweat, but she had lost her father and discovered deceit in her own family. While she didn't want to, she knew it was time to gear up for war.

During her time of reflection, Christie hadn't noticed that Michael had moved closer to the front door. Something took over her as she marched closer to him, cocked her hand back and prepared to let his face meet her fist. It wasn't what Christie had wanted, by any means, but she was tired of their games. Before she could follow through, though, she felt Junior's firm grip on her wrist.

"Come on, Chris," her cousin pleaded with his baby face in front of hers. She had always loved him but even so, there was no calming her down.

"Not like this," he said as he pulled her away from Michael.

"Not like what?" Christie shouted as she freed herself from his grip. Christie was sure the neighbors were listening and, in fact, she was hoping they were.

"Would it have been better if I was a thief in the night like them?" Christie screamed as she felt a tear on her cheek. She wasn't sure how long she had been crying or what had triggered her tears, but they were there and not showing any signs of slowing down.

Junior's expression revealed the sympathy he felt, but at the end of the day, Angelica was his mother and his loyalty was with her.

"The cops are coming, Chris. You need to leave."

The neighbors heard the word *cops* and started to whisper. This had be the most excitement in this neighborhood in years, Christie thought, as she wiped away a trail of tears.

Christie disregarded Junior's pleas and instead went right for the spot on the porch where Michael stood begging Angelica to unlock the front door. Christie bolted towards him, unable to contain her anger.

"I know that you are weak and have no backbone—you've always been that way—but tell that wife of yours I am nowhere near done with her. Whatever y'all are hiding will be exposed!" Christie screamed loudly.

Finally, Angelica unlocked the door and scurried back into the house. If someone had ever told Christie she would be standing in front of her aunt's house shouting, she would never have believed them—but here she was.

"And by the way, Michael," she said before he had a chance to step into the house, "I know all about Cleveland in '97."

Shaken by her words, Michael couldn't even find a response to fire back. Christie could see she had rattled him enough to ignite a bit of fear. At this point, Christie was fighting fire with fire; she had to prove to them she would definitely burn them if necessary.

"Chris," Junior said as he pointed in the direction of the sirens. As if shaken from a dream, Christie finally realized her aunt had *actually* called the cops on her.

"I can't believe this," Christie said as she put her key in the ignition and looked back up at Junior, "but you better believe what was done in the dark will definitely come to the light."

She pulled out of the driveway just as the police pulled in. Christie stopped to watch as Angelica ran out of the house like a distressed banshee, pointing and shouting for the police officers to follow, stop and arrest her niece.

Christie nodded her head. Everything *would* come to light; she just wondered how.

Five

Christie was fuming. She couldn't believe her "luck."

"I should go back and just let her have it," she yelled as she turned down a one-way street and found a parking spot.

"Chris, you need to chill," Junior said as he sat in the passenger seat looking over at his cousin.

It had all happened so fast. Christie had started out at Angelica's house and caused a scene but had gotten nowhere. She wasn't even sure how Junior wound up in the car with her or why, but there he was and she wasn't about to turn down his company. She'd hadn't planned on going to her aunt's house and having the cops called on her but, as she was discovering, her life was one big "build as you go" mess.

Since she had left Angelica's house, with an unforgettable run-in with Michael, there was nothing more that Christie could focus on besides finding out the truth.

"I don't need to do anything remotely close to chilling, Junior," Christie sighed. She could feel herself about to hyperventilate.

"What's going on? Why did you show up at my mom's house? You need to tell me something."

Although the car was still parked, Christie gripped the steering wheel tightly. Her eyes were glued to her windshield, as if it contained the answers to Junior's questions. The truth was, Christie did not trust her own thoughts and because of that she couldn't spill it all to Junior.

"Someone stole all of my father's money," Christie said, finally taking her eyes off the windshield. "*All* of his money," she repeated.

Junior frowned. "Are you serious?" he said in disbelief, "How do you know?"

Christie tried to keep herself calm. She had repeated the story so many times that she was tired of replaying the horrid details.

"I called to have his accounts frozen after his death and when I called today, they told me all he had in his account at the time of his death was $1,100," Christie said as she allowed more tears to trickle down her cheeks.

Even Junior knew how much of a stickler his Uncle Kenneth had been about money. Eleven hundred dollars couldn't have been all that was in his account and the shock on Junior's face told Christie that he knew this too.

"I can't believe…but…wait…why are you coming at mom and Aunt Evelyn like this?" Junior asked, finally piecing the puzzle together.

Christie turned her eyes back to the windshield. As much as it hurt her to accuse her aunts of having a hand in the theft, it hurt her even more to say so to Junior. Sure, he and his mother hadn't had the easiest relationship but she *was* his mother.

When Christie rolled her eyes, Junior spoke up.

"You think they had something to do with this, Chris?" he asked with skepticism.

Christie shrugged.

"Christie, do you hear yourself? Do you?" Junior asked loudly.

"You're saying your aunts—your father's sisters—stole from him? *You* can't even believe that."

Christie heard the hurt tone in her cousin's voice and that pained her heart.

"I know what my gut is telling me, Junior and that's all I know," Christie said matter-of-factly.

"I know who had access to the accounts at the time and I know what my father should have had in his account. Someone's lying and I'm going to find out the truth."

Junior looked as though his mind was about to explode with all this new information and he wondered how much more he could take.

"My mom wouldn't do anything like that and you know it. My mom has *always* been the most honest person I've ever known. Shoot, she even turned me in one time when I stole a gumball from the grocery store as a child," Junior mumbled.

Christie was listening but she wasn't trying to hear all of her cousin's rationales for why his so-called angelic mother was incapable of such a crime. She had already played the same explanations out in her mind before she settled on the fact that her father had been taken advantage of, while he was dying, by the people he trusted most.

"Christie, I'm not saying you're crazy or that *someone* isn't responsible for the missing money. I'm just saying I don't think my mom would have any part of something like that."

"Junior, both of them—Aunt Evelyn and Aunt Angelica—have been acting so strange to me since my father passed I can't even put it into words. Aunt Angelica had always been so outgoing and giving, even when she was acting snooty. And Aunt Evelyn, even when she was being a complete witch, was never *this* distant and mean."

Junior listened quietly and watched as his cousin vented. He could see the pain on her face.

"No one is keeping me in the loop about my own father's funeral, Junior. No one has asked for my input and when I try to give it, they shut me out. I've been trying to get answers on his finances and his funeral for days now. It's as if they want to act like they were all he had, but that's a lie. My father had me, my mother, his family and his friends. It's not right the way they're treating the rest of us," Christie said as a single tear rolled down her cheek. "It's like they want me to shut up and go in a corner to grieve, but I can't. That was my father, Junior, my *father*. When he died, a part of me died too and now I just want answers about things."

Junior exhaled and put his hand on top of Christie's. Usually he could lighten the mood with a joke or corny face, but right now he was drawing a blank. On one hand, his mother was being accused of stealing from her dying brother and on the other hand, his cousin was going through a range of emotions due to her father's death and her suspicions. He felt so conflicted about what to believe and what to do.

Christie wiped her face and shook herself out of her trance.

"But this isn't your battle to fight. I know Angelica's your mother and you have your loyalty to her," Christie said glancing over at him.

"My loyalty is to the *truth* and to *family,* the same as it's always been," he said as he rubbed her hand softly.

They were two of the closest cousins in the family so it was no surprise they relied on each other in times of need. And right then Christie needed an ear even more than she needed someone on her side.

"Oh shoot," Christie said as she eyed the time, "I need to call the funeral home. I've been trying to get in touch with Deborah or someone at the funeral home for several days."

Junior sat back and stared out of the passenger window while Christie dialed the number and sat with the phone to her ear.

"This is Christie Whitfield-Adams. I was looking to speak with someone about my father," Christie said.

Someone on the other end of the phone replied.

"Okay, do you know when someone will be available to speak to me? It's rather urgent."

Junior looked over at his cousin and raised an eyebrow.

"Ok, thanks," Christie said as she hung up.

"What happened?" Junior asked.

Christie shook her head, threw the car in drive and sucked her teeth.

"They're playing a game with me, Junior. I don't know exactly what's going on but I know when I'm being avoided. The same way your mom and Aunt Evelyn have been avoiding me, the funeral home and even Deborah, have been doing the same. Something isn't right," Christie said as she pulled into traffic, "and since they won't take my calls or call me back we're going to pay them a visit."

"You have to go in there calm and collected or they'll shut down, Chris," Junior explained as they barreled through traffic.

When they arrived at the funeral home, Junior had calmed Christie down.

"Calm and collected," Christie sighed as they got out of the car and headed toward the front of the building.

The Thomason Funeral Home was gorgeous. Immaculately designed, the outside looked more like a luxurious retirement home than a funeral home. The well-manicured landscape and fabulous brick that adorned the spacious building intimidated Christie. She hated funeral homes.

When they reached the over-sized wood door and pulled it open, Christie and Junior gasped at the expensive interior.

"This looks like something in one of those interior design magazines, Chris," Junior said as his voice echoed around the lobby.

Christie nodded in agreement as they made their way to what appeared to be the reception area.

"May I help you?" a woman asked as she appeared from a back room.

She was cute Christie thought to herself as she eyed the thirty-something woman who had deep chocolate skin and curly hair that accented her face.

"My name is Christie Whitfield-Adams and I just left a message about—" Christie started.

"Yes, Mrs. Adams. I remember speaking with you. No one has yet come in," the woman said defiantly as she sat in her chair and raised an eyebrow.

"And you're not sure when someone will be in?"

The woman looked at her computer, fidgeted with a few keys, and then looked up with a forced smile "No, I'm sorry."

Junior, sensing it was the time for him to act like a man, spoke up, "We just need to speak to someone about my uncle's arrangements."

"Like I told Mrs. Adams, no one is here right now who can assist you. Once someone returns, I will definitely have them call her," she replied, in a voice laced with attitude.

"Listen, miss, my uncle passed away unexpectedly and we're just trying to get everything pieced together. It's your job to make sure all of his arrangements are completed, right? So, again, I'm going to ask you to please point us in the direction of someone who can help," Junior said, his voice rising.

Christie placed her hand on his shoulder and whispered, "Calm and collected, remember?"

"Is Deborah around by chance?" Christie asked kindly.

"No. She's not here. I just said no one is here but me," the woman said as she punched numbers into her phone.

Within seconds, a large black man dressed in all black appeared from the back. He looked like he was a part of the maintenance crew and didn't seem pleased that he was interrupted.

"Mrs. Adams and her guest will be leaving now," the woman said to the burly man.

Christie was trying to make sense of what was happening. Were they being kicked out?

"What?" Christie asked as her eyes darted between the woman and the man.

"I'm going to ask that you all leave the premises."

"On what grounds?" Junior asked, getting angry.

"This is private property, sir. We have the right to ask anyone we'd like to leave."

Christie couldn't believe what was happening. They were asking all the right questions and getting all the wrong responses and it was starting to get even more confusing.

"Y'all need to leave now," the man repeated in a terrifying tone.

Christie didn't want to stick around to find out what they'd do if she or her cousin tried to object any further. Instead, she pulled on Junior's arm and led him away.

When they got in the car, Christie leaned back on the headrest and replayed the events in her head. It wasn't until Junior spoke that she realized it hadn't all been a dream.

"You're right, Chris, something's *not* right. I just don't know what it is. We should get some rest before your father's wake tonight."

Six

"Let me straighten your tie, baby," Christie said as she reached over and adjusted Anthony's dark blue tie.

"Thank you, sweetheart. How are you holding up today?" Anthony asked as his hands met hers and he rubbed them gently.

"I'm doing…okay, I guess. I don't think it's hit me that today I'm burying my father, you know?" Christie said as she turned away from her husband and took a deep breath.

Standing in their hotel room, Christie peered out over the city and tried to enjoy the beautiful scenery. Still, her mind kept going back to her father.

She felt Anthony's arms wrap around her body and she melted into him. When she was with her husband, it was as if nothing else mattered.

"What can I do?" he asked softly.

"Make all of this be a dream."

"We have two hours or so until the service starts, why don't you take a nap?" Anthony suggested as he tugged Christie towards the bed.

"Anthony," Christie said, "I don't have time to lie down. I have to make sure I'm dressed, you're dressed and my mom and…I have to make sure…"

Anthony held up one hand and silenced his wife.

"Everyone will be okay without you for thirty minutes. You're burying your father today, Chris. I think it's okay if you take some time for yourself."

Christie took a second and thought about what Anthony was saying. After that day she wouldn't have the luxury of going to see her father whenever she wanted to and that scared her.

"I want to go to the funeral home and spend one last moment alone with him if that's okay with you," Christie said without making eye contact. She was sure it sounded insane to want to be alone with a dead person, but she didn't care.

"Are you sure you and mom will be okay?" Christie asked as Anthony helped her make her way towards the door.

"We'll be fine. You just make it back in one piece before the service, baby," Anthony said as he placed the rental car keys in her hands.

As Christie drove towards the funeral home, silence played as her soundtrack. It was as if she knew she was driving but she *really* wasn't driving. Her hands were on the steering wheel and her feet were on the pedals, but her mind was everywhere but on the road.

As she stopped the car at a red light, she peered over at a bus stop and saw a little child bundled up sitting next to what appeared to be their parent. Christie smiled at the brown-faced, chubby-cheeked child.

"Daddy, why do you always have to bring up children? When Anthony and I are ready, I promise you and mom will be the first people we call," Christie had said as she played with her hair over dinner one evening a year earlier.

She and Anthony were still settling into being husband and wife, but that didn't stop her father from asking about grandchildren every chance he could.

"You're my only child, Christie. I want to spoil your children rotten and then send them back to you."

Christie laughed at her father's honesty.

"That's cold, Daddy, real cold."

The two sat in Kenneth's living room pigging out on lo mein, spring rolls, and chicken with broccoli and talking about everything under the sun.

"How's your mother doing?" Kenneth asked as he sipped from a glass of Voss sparkling water.

"She's doing pretty well. You know, staying busy at work and things. She asked about you the other day, too."

Kenneth smiled to himself for a second before returning to his food.

Christie had never asked but she knew her parents would always love each other. They had loved so intensely and passionately that even though they weren't together it was hard for them to fathom not loving one another.

"What's she say about grandchildren?" Kenneth asked playfully.

Christie rolled her eyes and sat down her fork.

"She's just as crazy as you are about them."

Kenneth's laughter echoed through the house and Christie finally joined in.

"I can just see you and Anthony now with a big-eyed baby running up and down these halls. Your mother and I will just sit back and laugh."

Christie shook her head at the thought and rolled her eyes.

"Is that what this is all about, Dad? So you can see how flustered your baby girl gets?" Christie joked.

Once Kenneth caught his breath, he sat back in his chair and crossed his arms. It was typical Kenneth fashion to go from joking to serious with the snap of a finger. Christie watched her father speak as his eyes darted off to nothing in particular.

"Actually, it's because I want to see what kind of values your mother and I have instilled in you that you're going to instill in your children. I have no doubt you're going to be a great mother when the time comes. No doubt at all."

Christie would usually follow the serious comment with something funny but this time she let the moment remain as it was.

"Thank you, Daddy."

"Besides, if you aren't a great mother, you know who I'll blame," Kenneth said as he laughed again and slapped his knee. "Your mother."

Christie felt tears stinging her cheek as she pulled into the funeral home and threw the car in park. Something felt final about this visit.

She stepped inside the funeral home and no one seemed to be around, which was perfect for Christie. As she opened the double doors that led to the chapel, she paused. While she could pretend it wasn't her father's wake yesterday evening and that she didn't have a horrible visit with Junior earlier that day, with all the hustle and bustle that had gone on, there was no way she could pretend about today.

Entering the chapel, Christie stood still as she looked at her father's open casket near the end of the aisle. She lifted her feet and walked closer, but it seemed like she was standing still. Forcing herself to keep her eyes open, Christie felt herself getting closer and finally began sobbing just as she approached the blue chrome casket.

"Blue always was your favorite color, Daddy," Christie said as she hesitantly reached in and touched her father's cold hand. Nothing had shaken her more than feeling her father's ice-cold skin. She wanted to make believe he was just asleep, just taking a long nap, but feeling his cold skin destroyed that fantasy and gave her the finality her heart didn't want to accept.

"Daddy…" Christie wept as she looked at her father's perfect face and took in all of his character and handsomeness, "Daddy, why?"

She wasn't expecting an answer and knew she would never get one, but she still had to ask exactly what was on her heart and mind.

There he lay in his dark blue, pinstriped suit with a white shirt and dark tie looking so peaceful. His hair was freshly cut and he looked to have a bit of a grin on his face. In some way, her father's grin brought her comfort that nothing else could.

"Daddy, I told you I was coming. I didn't even get a chance to say goodbye," Christie cried as her hands ran up and down her father's hand. It hurt her heart to think back to their last conversation—when she thought she had more time, but didn't.

"This is Christie," she answered the phone at her desk.

"Christie, this is Deborah. We need to talk," Deborah said with panic in her voice. Immediately, Christie could tell something was wrong. Why else would Deborah be calling her?

"What's going on? Is my father…is he okay?" Christie asked as tears formed in her eyes at the thought.

It had been a week since she had last seen her father, who was still in the hospital, and she was making immediate plans to get back to see him. He wasn't doing much better but, as far as Christie could tell, he wasn't getting worse either.

"Christie…he's…he's not doing well at all. Hold on, let me have you speak to the doctor." Christie heard a lot of rustling before a deep voice came on the phone.

"Hi, Mrs. Adams? I'm Doctor Ryan, I've been treating your father. How are you?"

Christie wasn't in the mood for formalities. If something was happening, she needed to know. "What's going on with my father?" Christie asked straightforwardly.

The doctor paused before answering as if he were choosing the appropriate words.

"We've done everything we can but Mr. Whitfield is progressively getting worse. His blood pressure has steadily been dropping and he refuses to eat."

"So what are you saying? Is there some sort of medicine you can give him or—"

"What I'm saying, Mrs. Adams, is that we've done all we can. I don't know if it will be days, weeks or months, but your father's condition is not improving and I wanted you, as his daughter, to know."

Christie felt like she'd had a ton of bricks dropped on her chest as she tried to make sense of everything being thrown at her.

"Are you saying…are you saying my father is dying?"

The doctor's lack of an answer spoke loudly enough to Christie who demanded to speak to her father.

"Daddy? How do you feel?" Christie asked as she tried to mask the fact that she was crying.

"I'm okay, baby girl. I feel a little sleepy today, but I'm hanging in there," Kenneth said as he coughed. Christie couldn't believe how different her father sounded. His normally booming and confident voice was now raspy and weak. Christie's heart dropped.

"Daddy, I'm coming to see you first thing tomorrow, okay? I have to book a flight and I'll be there tomorrow."

Christie could imagine her father smiling as he weakly said, "Okay, baby girl."

"Daddy, I love you," Christie said as she bit her bottom lip and tried to stay calm.

"I love you more, baby girl."

"I'll see you soon. Make sure you're doing everything they tell you to do."

"I'll see you soon, baby girl," her father repeated before passing the phone off to Deborah.

One hour later she had received a call that her father had passed away.

"Daddy, I was trying to get to you…I told you I would be there. I love you, Daddy," Christie wept as she laid her head on her father's cold chest. She knew he wasn't there and she knew all she was talking to was his shell but it still comforted her. Christie kissed her father on his forehead and quickly left the funeral home to meet back up with Anthony and her mother at the hotel.

Nothing could have prepared Christie for the twists and turns her life would take once her father's illness came to light but as she gripped her father's lifeless hand, none of those twists and turns mattered. She was just a little girl wanting to say one last goodbye to her father. She would think about the twists, turns and the deceit the next day.

Seven

Christie kicked her heels off at the door and slowly walked towards the familiar couch in her mother's front room.

"You okay, honey?" Anthony asked as he followed behind her and ran his hands over her tense shoulders.

Christie shrugged and dropped onto the couch. Her mother entered the room shortly afterwards and sat next to her daughter.

Hours earlier they had all done the hardest thing they'd ever had to do when they buried Kenneth. Alise had tried to hide her hurt but Christie could tell simply by her red eyes and puffy face that her mother had been crying long after the funeral ended.

"The service was…interesting," Alise said as she looked up at Anthony and widened her eyes.

Christie rolled her eyes and threw her head back on the couch.

Planning a funeral is never a joyous time but in Christie's mind the funeral itself should always be a celebration of life and not a reason to act ridiculous. Her mind wandered back to the previous morning when they all had gathered at the funeral home before the service, after she privately visited her father.

"There's Evelyn," Anthony said as they pulled into the parking lot.

"Hmph," Christie said as she applied another coat of deep red lipstick. The trio planned to drop their car at the funeral home and ride in one of the assigned family town cars to the church.

"Are you sure you're okay?" Alise asked as she looked at her daughter.

"I'm as okay as I'll ever be, Ma," Christie snapped.

She wasn't trying to be mean. She just wanted the day to be over.

As Christie, Anthony and Alise walked toward the funeral home, people looked in their direction but very few of them spoke.

"Why is everyone just staring at us?" Anthony asked in a whisper.

Christie shrugged her shoulders as she adjusted her dark shades. She had no intention of speaking to many people. She was burying her father, after all. But she did find it strange that people seemed to be going out of their way *not* to speak to her.

"Hey, Cuz," Junior said as he opened the doors and let her inside. She embraced her cousin and forced a smile.

"Hey Aunt Alise, Anthony. Good to see y'all," Junior said as he hugged them.

"I think we're about to load up in a few minutes. Y'all are just on time."

It baffled Christie that she seemed to be more of an outsider at her own father's funeral than anyone else. She had played it over and over in her mind and couldn't make sense of the fact that her aunts hadn't allowed her to be involved with any of the planning for the funeral. While some might have viewed it as one less stress, Christie found it to be another suspicion to tack onto her list.

"Just tell us where to go," Christie said as she eyed her aunts entering the hallway headed towards her. Christie felt her body tense up as she squeezed Anthony's hand tightly. She hadn't been nervous or even afraid to see her aunts, but she was interested to see their reaction to seeing her.

Christie kept her eyes on the two of them as they appeared to be talking so deeply they didn't even notice their niece standing before them. Alise was the first to speak.

"Evelyn. Angelica," Alise said as she cleared her throat.

"Hi…hi…" Angelica stuttered as she looked at the group of people standing inside the lobby.

Christie wondered if her aunt was concerned about the scene they might make or if she was genuinely surprised to see them.

Evelyn's and Christie's eyes locked. Removing her shades, Christie stared at her aunt so intently it seemed like the room went silent.

She wanted to ask her why and she wanted a real answer. She wanted her aunts to be honest and explain exactly what happened and how their once tightly knit family was now holding on by a thread. Christie wondered if her eyes were delivering the questions to her aunt.

When Evelyn and Angelica proceeded past their niece and family without a hug or an acknowledgement, Christie guessed everyone else knew something was up.

"I can't believe them," Alise said as they headed outside to the town cars.

"Chris, Aunt Alise and Anthony, y'all are in the first car. If it's okay with you, y'all will be the only ones in the car."

Christie narrowed her eyes to better understand what her cousin was saying.

"Usually it's all of the immediate family in the first car, Junior. Why are we the only ones in here?" Christie asked. "No one wants to ride with us?"

Junior took a deep breath telling them everything they needed to know.

"That's fine by us. We don't want to ride with anyone who doesn't want to ride with us," Christie said loudly as she slid into the black car. Anthony and Alise followed and sat quietly inside while the rest of the family loaded up in the other cars.

"I just can't believe this," Alise said. "Kenneth wouldn't have wanted it like this."

Christie leaned her head against the window and watched as people scurried to their own cars or the other town cars. This *wasn't* how her father would've wanted things but, she rationalized, no one had asked her for any input so she wasn't about to give it now.

As the car drove off, Christie put her sunglasses back over her eyes. The sun was shining brightly and while Christie normally loved beautiful days, she was in no mood to celebrate. She watched as the world passed by.

"They didn't even want to ride with us," she said softly as Anthony's hand reached over and caressed hers.

Christie had taken the drive along the route from the funeral home to the church so many times she knew the landmarks like the back of her hand. Still, on that day it was like everything was brand new. The old corner store that she'd passed a million times looked more intriguing and the tattered restaurant that served old-school burgers, malts and shakes now looked like it was full of character. Christie was taking in the same-old-same-old with new eyes; it was refreshing.

"It's a beautiful day, though. They can't take that away. Daddy told me he was born on a beautiful afternoon. He said grandma told him the sun was shining so hard she didn't have a choice but to have him on that day. Grandma told daddy that the day he was born was one of the most beautiful days ever. Kind of ironic that the day we're burying him is just as beautiful as she described, right?" Christie rambled as she ran her manicured fingernails over the wood-grained door.

"Your father was a beautiful man, Christie. He wouldn't have had his funeral day anything less than beautiful," Alise said as she dabbed her eyes.

Christie often wondered how her mother actually felt about her father's death. Yes, they were divorced but the connection between the two of them, even as friends, surprised most people. Christie sometimes wondered if they were soul mates that simply couldn't be together. Their love was amazing.

"You're right," Christie replied as she laid her head back on the window and closed her eyes.

Before she knew it, they were at the church. As they pulled around the side of the building, everyone climbed out of the cars and began to line up in the vestibule of the church.

"You're going to go here," one of the organizers said as he checked a paper and stood Christie, Anthony and Alise behind Evelyn, Angelica and their families.

"Wait…I'm his *daughter*. I don't go behind his sisters and their children," Christie said loudly.

Evelyn and Angelica looked at each other and coolly rolled their eyes.

"This is just according to the list we received from the family," the worker replied nervously. "If there's a change, we can definitely handle that."

"What family? *I'm* his family. I'm his daughter and I'm his next of kin. I'm supposed to walk out first," Christie said politely as she looked over at her aunts and then back to her mom and husband.

"Whatever's best," Angelica said as Evelyn eyed her sister angrily.

Christie couldn't believe her ears. They were really about to try to make her stand behind them and their family when she was her father's only child. She was the one who had been his heart and had given him inspiration to achieve and excel. She had been the one who loved her father with so much emotion and tenacity that it frightened her. She had been the spitting image her of father and they wanted her to play second fiddle, like she hadn't been his world?

"Okay. Come on, ma'am. Let's move you three to the front and we'll ask everyone else to just move back a few steps so we have enough room," the funeral worker announced in a stern tone.

Christie's head was spinning and she was fuming. The audacity of them to leave her out of the planning of her father's funeral and then act as though she didn't deserve to represent him as the first person walking out was maddening.

The music sounded, alerting Christie to make her first steps into the church. She looked around at familiar and unfamiliar faces and tears immediately began to stream down her face. Anthony gripped her hand tightly and she took a deep breath as she walked towards her father's casket.

"Oh, Daddy," Christie moaned softly as she ran her hand over his chest and face. She didn't care that he was ice cold or that she had seen him earlier that morning. The only thing that mattered was this would be the last time she would see her father.

After paying her respects at the casket, Christie headed to the first pew and took a seat. She could hear loud moans, cries and sniffles and she just wanted it all to be over.

Once everyone was seated, Christie took a deep breath and prepared for the service. That's when it happened.

"Close my brother's casket NOW!" Christie heard Evelyn yell.

Christie looked to her right and saw her aunt leave the pew and head towards the casket. Christie and Anthony stood up and moved to the front of the casket as well.

"What in the world are you doing?" Christie said through gritted teeth. The funeral workers were swarming them as Angelica joined the huddle as well.

"Evelyn wants to close the casket. She…we all…think it's too hard to keep it open any longer than it has to be."

Christie jerked her head to the side and tried her best to remain calm. This was her father's *funeral* not an episode of Maury.

"We are leaving the casket open until the program calls for it to be closed, okay?" Christie said adamantly.

Evelyn ignored her niece and turned to the funeral worker. "I want his casket closed. NOW!"

Christie looked over at Anthony and cleared her throat. "I am his next of kin and that casket is going to stay open until it would normally be closed. If you don't want to look at him—your baby brother—one last time, then close your eyes. If anyone has a problem with it, you can take it up with me after the service. Right now, though, have some decency and let my father's service be peaceful."

Christie didn't even wait for anyone to reply as she headed back to her seat.

The casket stayed open.

The preacher began speaking about death and how to be sure you're living your life to the best of your ability as Christie tried not to stress over the fact that her aunts seemed determined to ruin her father's funeral. He was talking about her father's accolades and telling funny stories when Christie thought she would lose her mind because suddenly her Aunt Evelyn began screaming. It wasn't that she didn't expect people to be sad about her father's passing; it was that she didn't expect it to be such a blatant show.

Evelyn whooped and hollered as if someone was pulling all of her teeth out, one by one. "Oh Lord, take me, Father. Give me back my brother. Oh, Lord!" Evelyn shouted so loud the pastor even stopped preaching.

"Oh, that was *my* brother. Oh Lord!" Evelyn carried on.

It wasn't until Christie gave her aunt a "stop playing" look that she toned it down. It was eerie to Christie that the times she glanced in the direction of her aunts she saw what seemed to be a sly grin on her Aunt Evelyn's face.

As they neared the end of the service and people stood up to talk about Kenneth, Christie couldn't take her eyes off the grin on Evelyn's face. It seemed as if she was getting a sick satisfaction out of the funeral itself.

"Do you see her?" Christie whispered to Anthony who looked over and shook his head.

"Something's not right with her today." Anthony said.

"When is it ever right?" Christie shot back.

Anthony shrugged.

One of her father's former colleagues stood and gave a beautiful speech about how Kenneth had influenced him to become a great man. Things like that touched Christie and made her remember that, despite all of her aunt's efforts, her father was loved, appreciated and revered. It was truly the only way she was able to remain sane through her father's funeral.

Christie found herself reflecting more than crying. She missed her father more than she could vocalize but was determined to figure out what happened to his money and who was behind it.

Leaving the burial site, Christie, Anthony and Alise got inside of the town car and headed back to the church for the repast.

"I'm starving," Anthony said as he loosened his tie a little bit.

"Me too, but I have a headache. Do you think we can stop at a gas station to get some aspirin?" Christie asked the driver, who agreed.

Christie ran in and grabbed the first packet of aspirin she could find.

"Is this all, pretty girl?" the older black man at the register asked with a wink.

Christie smiled and nodded.

"You're Kenneth's little girl, aren't you? I haven't seen you around here in years," the man said as he rang up her aspirin. "I sure was sorry to hear about your father. He was such a nice man."

Christie had forgotten she'd practically grown up in that gas station, going for candy and juice when she visited her father. With everything going on, it hadn't even dawned on her that this was the gas station.

"Thank you," Christie said, "we're all pretty shaken up."

Christie fumbled with her billfold and pulled out a five dollar bill.

"No, no. It's on the house."

Christie smiled, took her aspirin and headed towards the door.

"Thank you, sir," she said as she looked around the small building and remembered running up and down the aisles when she was young and visiting her father. She could close her eyes and see her father standing there with his hands on his hips laughing at her excitement about all of the candy.

"You're welcome, pretty girl."

When Christie arrived at the repast, she was feeling better. Maybe it was the aspirin or maybe it was the friendly man who had reminded her of a forgotten memory of her father. Memories of her father were starting to be her personal favorites.

"And I'd like to say…" Christie heard her Aunt Evelyn saying over a microphone as she, Anthony and Alise entered the room.

"What's going on?" Alise asked Junior who was standing near the entrance.

"Aunt Evelyn is giving a thank you speech."

Christie rolled her eyes and listened. She was already annoyed that she hadn't been included and made to feel like an outsider. And now her aunt was finding yet another way to exclude her.

"Kenneth was my baby brother," Evelyn said as she dabbed some non-existent tears from her face, "and I'm going to miss him. Angelica and her family, me and my family and, of course, the entire Whitfield clan is going to miss that smile. It's been a long week since we lost him but every day we get stronger. Thank God," Evelyn said as she looked at Christie.

"Kenneth was a son, a brother, a colleague and a great friend to all."

Christie felt like someone was reaching into her heart and slowly ripping it from her chest. It hurt to be disregarded in front of everyone, but she did it with a smile.

"I'm ready to leave," Christie whispered to Anthony as Evelyn continued to ramble.

"Are you sure, baby? We just got here and we want to make sure we thank everyone who came."

Alise rubbed her daughter's back and tried to calm her down.

"They aren't even acknowledging that I'm his child and the only piece of Kenneth Whitfield that's left. I want to go."

Christie zoned out on the ride to the funeral home and then on the ride back to her mother's house. She wanted to make sense of why her aunts were acting as if she didn't exist but she was finding it hard to get past the hurt.

"Don't let it upset you," Alise said as they all sat on the couch and exhaled.

"I'm past being upset. Now I'm just determined. They don't even realize what they've done. Instead of making me run away, they've fueled my curiosity."

"They've always been like this, even when your father and I were married. They were really protective of Kenneth and felt like I was taking their time with their brother. They've always been jealous of anyone who entered the picture and jeopardized the control they had over Kenneth."

Christie shook her head. "Even me? I'm his daughter—their niece."

Alise nodded, "Even with you. You were still a threat."

Christie dropped her head into her hands and contemplated her next move. She could easily just let everything slowly come to light or she could force the truth to show itself sooner rather than later.

Lifting her head out of her hands, Christie smirked.

"Well, they haven't felt what it feels like to be threatened."

Eight

Christie stared at the slop in front of her and took a deep breath. She knew Anthony meant well but if it didn't involve his famous lasagna, they both knew he didn't belong in a kitchen.

"What is it?" Christie asked playfully as she poked the brown meaty lump on her plate with her fork.

Anthony laughed heartily as he shook his head.

"Don't talk about my cooking like that, Christie. Just taste it. I bet you fall in love with it."

Christie doubted that. She'd had Anthony's mystery pasta, his fried-but looks baked-chicken and his spicy tuna concoction and she had hated all of them. Still, she appreciated everything he was doing to try to make her feel better.

Picking up a chunk of the mystery meat and placing it in her mouth, Christie grimaced as her taste buds finally realized that this was not a delicious meal.

"Babe," Christie said as she swallowed the small amount and quickly took a swig of water.

"I can't eat this." She said with a slight grin.

Anthony stared at his plate and Christie's and started laughing.

"You were better than me. I wasn't even going to taste it!" Anthony kidded as he scooped both of their plates up just as Christie reached over to pinch him for his prank.

"I'm starving, though." Christie whined.

"I'm going to run out and get some food. Do you want Subway?"

Christie shrugged and took a deep breath. Before she knew it Anthony was out of the door with her usual order request in tow.

As her mouth salivated over the thought of a delicious sub, Christie heard her stomach growl. She hadn't been this hungry and starved for real food since the day she'd overheard the unthinkable.

Christie's stomach growled as her mind wandered back to that day.

Christie had been at the hospital all day. The last thing she wanted to do was spend another hour there while her father slept. She needed real food, she needed to watch television without volume or station limitations and, most of all, and she just needed to get out of the hospital. Her father had been stabilized but from her standpoint he had a long ways to go.

Christie took a cab to Aunt Evelyn's house because her aunt had mistakenly picked up her keys earlier that day, leaving Christie stranded at the hospital.

As soon as she rested, bathed and ate, she would get the rental keys from her aunt and head back to the hospital.

She settled into the living room couch, setting her drink on the hardwood floor as she stretched out to watch television.

"Oh look, the Cosby show is on," Christie said to herself as she unfolded a foot-long Subway sandwich she'd picked up on the way home.

She only had a few more days at her aunt's house and with her father before she had to head back home to Anthony. She missed her husband badly, but she felt horrible about leaving her father.

"Baby girl, you know I'll be okay if you go home. You have a husband now. I can't be your first priority," Kenneth had said one day while they were eating lunch together.

Christie had come to enjoy the time they spent together talking about life.

"I know, Daddy, but Anthony understands. Right now, you are my first priority," Christie said as she stirred a bowl of chicken noodle soup.

Kenneth stopped her and forced her to look him in the face. Christie was used to seeing her father serious, but this was a different type of seriousness. His face was stern and there wasn't an ounce of humor to be found.

"You remember your husband is your priority. You take care of Anthony. He's a good man. One of the biggest mistakes I made was thinking that your mom came after my mom. Your spouse comes right after God," Kenneth said.

It was one of the few times Christie had heard her father speak regretfully about losing her mother as his wife.

"Okay, Daddy," Christie said as she patted his hand and calmed him down. The last thing she wanted to do was upset him.

As Bill Cosby made some goofy joke to Rudy on television, Christie found herself forgetting all about her issues at the hospital and laughing at the television show she had grown up loving. Something about the normalcy of Bill Cosby made her feel like everything would be all right. Even when she grew old enough to know the Cosby family was fictional, they still made Christie feel safe.

Just as she started admiring Claire Huxtable's beauty, Christie heard keys in the door and made a quick decision to turn the television off and remain quiet. She didn't feel like talking to her aunt so she pretended to be asleep.

"Evelyn, you need to fix this and you need to fix it now. This isn't right!" Christie heard a voice that sounded like her Aunt Angelica say.

Immediately, Christie knew she wasn't supposed to hear what she was hearing. There was conflict in the air and rather than miss it, Christie decided to stay quiet and learn what she could.

"It's done, Angelica. You can either tell him to go along with it or not. I don't care!" Evelyn shouted back at her sister.

Christie heard them moving from the hallway to the kitchen. Thankfully because of how the couch was situated, they had no idea she was laying on it listening to them argue.

"You can't do this, Evelyn. That's my son!" Angelica yelled as she slammed something down on the kitchen counter.

In all her life, Christie had never heard her aunts argue with one another. Christie knew from discussions with her father that they didn't always see eye to eye, but she couldn't imagine them going at each other's throats.

"Listen, you knew what this was all about when we agreed to make this move, Angelica. Don't try to get all self-righteous on me now. Junior can be in or he can be out but his name stays there."

"You've done a lot of dumb things in your life, Evelyn, and every time I've been there to pick up the pieces and tell you it can be fixed. This can't be fixed. Yes, I knew what we were doing but I didn't agree to involve Junior in this."

There was an awkward silence before Evelyn spoke.

"It's too late," she said softly. "The paperwork is in. If we change things now people will get suspicious. It has to stay. Kenneth would have a fit; you know that. But we're doing what's right for him and for us."

Christie knew that tone. It was the same one Evelyn used on her when she was a child and her aunt wanted to coax her into doing something. The same tone she used when she was being phony.

"This isn't right, Evelyn. If this comes back on Junior and he gets in trouble, he'll never forgive me and I'll never forgive you," Angelica wailed.

Her aunt was crying. Christie lay motionless on the couch, frozen by fear. This wasn't some ordinary argument over who used the last of the sugar. This was serious.

"Calm down, Angelica, just calm down. You're being so dramatic, as usual," Evelyn said as she sucked her teeth.

"I'm being dramatic? Do you understand what you just told me could land all of us, including Junior, in a lot of trouble? What am I going to tell Michael about his wife and son?" Angelica asked as she choked up.

"You can tell him whatever you want. It's not as if he's getting nothing out of it, Angelica. Besides, Junior isn't even his son. Stop being so dramatic."

The words caused Christie to gasp. She'd heard rumors before that Junior was the result of an affair Angelica had early in her marriage. To hear confirmation made her sick to her stomach. What else had they been hiding? She knew it was technically none of her business, but she felt betrayed. Did Junior know? Had that been the reason he had drawn away from his mother years earlier? Questions swirled around in Christie's mind as she heard her Aunt Angelica crying loudly.

"How dare you bring up something like that right now, Evelyn? You, of all people, with all the things you've done and all the schemes you've been a part of, are going to throw that in my face?" Angelica shouted loudly. Gone were the tears, Christie now heard only anger in her aunt's voice.

"For your information, he is Michael's son, regardless of whether or not he's his biological son. It sounds like you're a little bitter about the fact that you could never keep a decent man around long enough to even want to have a baby with you," Angelica said with attitude.

There were a few minutes of silence before Christie heard her aunts attempting to whisper.

"Is she here?" Angelica asked quietly.

"I didn't see her car. She must still be at the hospital," Evelyn replied before continuing. "You have to watch how you're talking so loudly coming into my house, Angelica. You never know when she's going to be here and what she'll hear."

Before Christie could lean closer to hear more, she heard footsteps coming towards the couch.

"Call me when you get home. We'll talk about this later," Evelyn said as she escorted her sister to the front door.

"Fine, but this has to change. Junior's name has to come off. All of our hands have to be clean," Angelica replied.

"I'll see what I can do," Evelyn said nonchalantly. "I'm about to go back up to the hospital. We need to be seen there as much as possible."

Christie heard her aunt's key in the door as she locked up and left. As quickly as the voices had entered the house, they were gone and Christie was left with more meaningless facts than she cared to have. Little did she know the facts she didn't want to have would turn out to be the facts she couldn't move forward without.

Nine

Christie laughed to herself, although nothing was particularly funny. For close to ten years, including her experience as an intern, her life as a reporter had been solely about finding the juicy story and reporting on it. As she caught a glimpse of herself on the security camera, she saw the irony in her situation. While her family troubles weren't exactly newsworthy to anyone outside her family, the irony of her own life seeming like a Lifetime movie humored her. Though it had only been a few months since her father passed away, it felt like a few years. The weight of worry, stress and confusion had certainly started to wear her down.

Smoothing out her shirt and slacks, Christie took a deep breath. There were moments when she wanted to feel sorry for herself, but she couldn't. Questions wouldn't get answered if she spent the whole day feeling pitiful. Besides, Christie rationed, she was used to pressure and thrived on it. When she'd first started in news she lived for the rush of deadlines, putting the pieces together and being the best at what she did. Now it was different. Now the pressure she was feeling wasn't from the stress of deadlines or piecing together stories; it was her real life. The unfamiliarity of it all caused her to question everything and, more importantly, everyone.

"Good evening," the petite front desk clerk said in a chipper tone from behind the cherry wood counter. Neatly dressed in a bright yellow blouse that accented her cleavage, she politely smiled and waited for Christie to acknowledge her presence.

Christie was in a daze as she stared around the contemporarily decorated television station that had been recently renovated. It wasn't that she was shell-shocked, she was just dazed. As her mom would often put it, she had too many thoughts and not enough time to sort through them all.

Excusing herself to grab the ringing phone, the receptionist smiled widely as she picked up the line. Quickly transferring the call, the girl opened her mouth to speak to Christie, but was interrupted by the lobby door opening.

"Hello Alice," a nice-looking man greeted as he slid his keycard over the pad on the front desk.

"Good evening," she replied with a bright, yet telling, smile.

It wasn't until she heard the receptionist's voice that Christie snapped out of her daydream. Somehow, amidst all of her swarming thoughts as she entered the lobby, Christie had not noticed the young woman. In fact, she couldn't even recall getting out of her car—or even the drive to the station for that matter. Floating through life had become the norm for her.

With a painted-on smile, Christie spoke, "I'm sorry, I was in another world."

"It's okay, we've all been there," the receptionist said with a playful exhale.

Christie wanted to compliment the young woman on her green eye shadow but wasn't sure if she should be encouraging her, applauding her or helping her pick out a new color. Christie was a natural beauty who rarely had to rely on many colors and schemes to get attention so she stared at the Jolly-Rancher-green eye shadow in front of her, a bit amazed. A part of her also wondered whose niece this was working the front desk.

"How may I help you?" she asked Christie.

"I have an appointment with Janice Goldberg," Christie replied. The young woman punched in numbers on the phone and leaned over to see a very charming older man entering the lobby. The man looked like he was a head honcho of sorts, someone who carried a high position, and Christie could tell the receptionist was smitten.

Christie shook her head and reached for the sign-in sheet, where she followed the instructions to provide her name, contact person, reason for visit and time. Finishing her signature with a curve at the end of the 's' and above the 'a' in one swoop was a technique she had been practicing for two weeks.

"Christie Whitfield-Adams," she said in a whisper as she looked over her signature with more thought than required of a woman who was getting ready to celebrate her third anniversary to a man she had nearly lost to pride. There was no question, she loved Anthony more than she could put into words and the last several months had proven that nothing could break their bond. Yet she was still nervous about the future and whether the past could ever be put to rest.

After reviewing the sign-in sheet, the young woman offered Christie a visitor's badge and directions to the waiting area. Christie politely listened to the instructions through a campaign of thoughts, fully aware of the turns she needed to take to her destination.

Since she was a little girl, Christie had learned how to stay in the shadows and today was no different. She had no interest in running into any of her former colleagues. There was no bad history between them, she merely did not want to walk down the 'let's catch up' corridor where people weaved their resumes into greetings like architects designing state-of-the-art facilities. All she wanted to do was get to the truth. It seemed simple enough yet, in reality, it was anything but that.

The busy movement of cameras and lights, and the commotion behind the chatter of local and national news, always gave Christie a high. There was something about knowing what others only suspected, or had no indication of, that she found euphoric.

She viewed the field of journalism as a world of its own. A place where rules were defined in hiding and admittance was only given to a select group. It was here that men and women were presented in shades and tones that declared their guilt or innocence. It was where adjectives sparked emotions that led to protest and lifestyle changes. Some found it inviting and addictive, while others saw it as the downfall of man. Christie, like many lovers of news, loved its thrills and despite its danger, could never imagine a life without it.

She stood in the shadows of the KTL Indianapolis studio waiting for Janice Goldberg, the evening news anchor and her long-time friend. Goldberg, a twenty-year veteran, had an ageless beauty. Her long legs, moderate curves, full brunette hair and wide eyes gave no indication of sleepless nights. Neither was it apparent that she was a woman who had worked her way to the top despite the gender-biased ruthlessness for which journalism was known.

Janice was a tough but fair cookie, known for getting answers that other seasoned reporters could not retrieve. On the streets, informants knew Janice would not give up a source because early in her career she had gone to jail for three months for refusing to reveal her source in a huge water scandal involving one of the city's top planning commissioners. Goldberg was the real deal.

Meeting at KTL nearly ten years ago, when Christie interned for Janice straight out of college, they had developed a relationship that extended beyond casual co-workers. They had become confidantes and, at times, co-conspirators. Goldberg knew she could trust Christie and had on many occasions turned to her dear friend. Although they didn't speak every day, their friendship held memories near and dear to them both.

Watching Janice wrap up the evening news, Christie couldn't help but smile at her friend, who had just hammered a local charity that was anything but charitable.

"I didn't know you were coming by the station tonight," said a robust voice from the shadows.

"And there is a reason for that," Christie replied flatly.

"Are you still playing hard to get Christie? You aren't going to be pretty forever," Channing Calhoun commented.

Channing was one of those friends that you loved to hate and hated to love. He and Christie had often flirted and in the next breath fought like siblings. Their relationship was strange but it made sense to them. When Christie first started at KTL they had tried dating but, as with most relationships in the newsroom, it sizzled then failed. Still, they kept their friendship strong and playful.

"Maybe not, but seeing how your career is going, you might want to get a little work done yourself," replied Christie.

Without missing a beat Channing chimed, "So you follow my career?"

"Of course. Everyone needs a daily dose of laughter," Christie stated.

Enjoying their banter, Channing and Christie did not notice Janice's approach.

"So why don't you just admit that you are in love with me," pleaded Channing.

"Well, well, look at the two of you. How do you always seem to find each other?" teased Janice.

"Don't you get started," hissed Christie.

Unable to contain their laughter Janice and Channing let out a thunderous roar.

"Come on Chris, you know you want to laugh," Janice said.

"You two are a mess!" Christie stated.

"Well what do you expect?" said Channing.

"This place can get a little stuffy, Chris," Janice added.

Seeing that Christie was struggling with whatever brought her to the station, Janice kissed Channing on the cheek and pulled Christie away.

"Hey," yelled Channing, "you *do* look good Chris!"

Ignoring his comment, Christie continued to walk with Janice who was tickled by Channing's outburst. "You know he's still in love with you, don't you?"

"Still? Channing has never loved anything or anyone like he loves Channing," responded Christie.

"Yes, that's true," Janice replied with a smirk.

The two women walked arm in arm until they reached Janice's dressing room, a lovely 250-square-foot space decorated more like a loft than a place for hair and make-up. Janice had insisted on decorating the place herself and had taken great pride in her collection of rare news articles that framed the walls. She had an original print from Waco, Texas, and another from the toppling of the Berlin Wall. Christie knew that news had always been in Janice's blood.

Quickly undressing, Janice put her finger to her lips, giving Christie the signal to not speak. As usual, Janice was working on a story that would shake the town and, as she always stressed, she never knew what ears were listening.

"Well, you just let me know when I can speak," Christie laughed as she sat quietly in the corner and watched the small television.

"Real funny, Chris," Janice said as she buttoned up her jeans.

Once outside her dressing room, Janice saw the bags under Christie's eyes and how thin her face had become, and knew the funeral couldn't be the only thing taking a toll on her friend. She knew Christie better than that, so something had to be up. Especially if Christie was willing to step a foot back in the station.

When Christie had discovered the secrets her aunts had been hiding about her father's finances, life as she knew it ceased to make sense. It had been four months since she'd confronted what she knew to be the truth and demanded answers. Since her father's passing, Christie was trying to gather the pieces with her head held high.

As usual, Janice needed to get to the bottom of the story, by any means.

Ten

"You have *got* to be kidding me," Evelyn snapped into the phone. "No, I don't want to leave a message. Tell her I need to speak with her immediately!" "She had better get on this phone," Evelyn muttered to no one in particular as she waited for her sister Angelica to come to the phone.

"I'm sorry Ms. Robinson, but Mrs. Harrison is not available at this time. I'll be more than happy to take a message," replied Hanna, Angelica's housekeeper.

Placing her hand over her chest and continuing to pace, Evelyn knew that Hanna couldn't make her spoiled little sister come to the phone and she really didn't want to cross Hanna, who had the power to easily make her calls go directly to voicemail. Hanna had at least been kind enough to answer the phone and try to get Angelica to take her calls.

Evelyn had been calling nonstop for three days. Each time she phoned, Angelica was unavailable. Yesterday she could hear Hanna in the background telling Angelica it sounded like an emergency. Angelica, on the other hand, had no interest in taking her call and was bold enough to tell Hanna just that.

"Hanna," Evelyn said with as much niceness as she could muster, "tell my dear sister that my lawyer will be calling her tomorrow and for her own good she should take the call."

"Yes, will do!" Hanna replied with a mix of nervousness and excitement. Evelyn wasn't sure if the housekeeper was happy or concerned that her employer was in trouble. Everything was a blur for her. It had all happened so quickly that she hadn't had a chance to catch her second wind. Frustrated and tired, Evelyn hung up the phone, turned on the gospel station and walked to the kitchen with a lone tear running down her face.

Angelica Harrison considered herself a good church-going woman who had served her family and community for nearly forty years. She often took in family members and strangers who needed a place to stay and had given tirelessly to her church. There was not a civic organization in Chicago that had not asked her to serve on their board or judge one of their many pageants or essay contests. But lately she had little to no interest in the things she loved or the energy required to put out recent fires.

Still fuming over the fact that her sister wouldn't stop calling, Angelica searched her pantry for ingredients. The stress of everything made her want to cook a huge meal for no reason at all. For Angelica, cooking had always been the way to create a bit of calm in the midst of any storm. She gathered the ingredients for potato salad, string bean casserole, fresh fried corn, macaroni and cheese, homemade yeast rolls, collard greens, peach cobbler, pineapple upside-down cake and her famous brown sugar honey glazed ham.

One would think a woman who loved to cook as much as she did would have some extra meat on her bones but, even in her early 60s, Angelica could still fit into her size eight wedding gown. She was, in fact, never without a compliment or admiring glance from men and women.

Pouring herself a large glass of white wine, Angelica began peeling potatoes as Michael, her husband of thirty-eight years came into the kitchen holding a beautiful bouquet of flowers that danced with Angelica's favorite shades of purple and lavender.

"Hey you," said Michael as he leaned in to kiss Angelica on the cheek.

"You're home early," she replied without acknowledging the flowers.

"I finished up a little early," he said as he reached for a vase, "just to spend time with you."

"You're so sweet, Michael. It's probably one of the main reasons I married you."

"That and my good looks, huh?" Michael asked with a raised eyebrow.

"Evelyn called *again*," she stated flatly.

"I know," Michael responded.

"What do you mean *you know*?" questioned Angelica.

"She called me at work today and said you were ducking and dodging her and suggested that I see about your mental stability," he sheepishly said as he popped a grape in his mouth.

"What?!" she screamed holding the carving knife in midair.

"She called *you*? I can see that we need to take a trip to see Ms. Thing because if she thinks for one minute I'm answering to *her* after all of this, then she has me sadly mistaken."

Watching his words, Michael continued as he took Angelica into his arms, "Angel, this will all blow over. You and Evelyn did nothing wrong. You know that men will bring false accusations against God's people but in the end God's people will always win. Sweetheart, you are a woman of the highest God and all of these lies will be revealed for what they are- lies. I promise that once your name is clear, we are going to get that ungrateful heifer—sorry, please excuse me, I know it's your family…"

"Family, now there is one for you," muttered Angelica as she wiped tears from her eyes and rested her head on Michael's shoulder.

"Why me Lord? Why me?" she cried out dramatically.

Seeing the two of them together would make the average person laugh. Angelica with her dramatic antics and over the top holier-than-thou act and Michael with his less than desirable looks and larger than average bank account; one would have to snicker. Michael had never been much of a looker, even Angelica would admit. When they first met close to forty years earlier, Angelica hadn't cared about anything Michael had to say, let alone that he was interested in her. Still, Michael was persistent and soon sent a town car to, literally, sweep Angelica off her feet on their first date. Many people said Angelica had married Michael for money, not for love, and she had never refuted the claim.

"I *do* love Michael," Angelica had whined over dinner one evening with her family after they'd announced their engagement. They saw through her and, more importantly, she knew they saw through her. Still, she was going to ride this lie out as long as possible, especially when it came with a family that was wealthy. Michael, who had been in law enforcement for more than twenty-five years, had recently retired from the force after being injured. However, his family name had carried them far. His parents, Dawson and Gloria Harrison, had started a very successful construction company in Chicago that was responsible for almost half of the downtown buildings and high-rises. To say they were well off would be an understatement. Michael had grown up much more privileged than Evelyn or Angelica, and money didn't mean much to him.

"Angelica, that man is…" Evelyn said with caution.

"Watch your mouth. That's my fiancé you're talking about," Angelica said as she peered at the five-karat engagement ring nestled on her left hand.

She had convinced herself that she loved him—all of him—even though she hadn't ever really been attracted to him physically. He had an odd look about him with oversized eyes, droopy lips and an awkward walk. Still, they had made it work for thirty-eight drama-filled years.

Soaking in the silence of their thoughts, Angelica went back to preparing their evening meal and Michael sorted through the stack of mail that had been gathering on the table, when he came upon a letter from Lillie Ann Sisters (LAS) Incorporated, a women's group that dated back to the early 1960s. This group of gifted women mentored young unwed mothers from the south side of Chicago and had a long-standing commitment to service in the community that had earned them a very respectable reputation.

Louise, the past president of LAS, had stepped down due to health reasons a few months ago and since that time Angelica has been the acting president. Under Angelica's leadership, the organization was able to double the fundraising from their annual silent auction, attended by the who's who of Chicago. Determined to make her mark, Angelica used her connections throughout the city to get auction donations that included tickets to the symphony, floor seats to the Bulls game against the Los Angeles Lakers and a personal chef for six months from LaBella Restaurant. After the success of the auction, all the big names in the organization thought Angelica should be the new president. It was only a matter of the upcoming election.

"Angel, you have a letter from LAS," Michael said as he rose from his seat at the breakfast nook and reached over toward the ham in front of him.

"Stop right there, mister," Angelica playfully said as he attempted to steal a sliver of ham.

"I love you my dearest Angel! Oh Angel! Oh Angel!" he sang as he kissed her neck and reached behind her for a piece of ham.

"I don't know how long you think that line is going to work on me," she said as she took the letter from him and stepped out of his embrace.

"Well," Michael said with a mouth full of ham, "is it still working?"

Trying to contain her laughter Angelica shook her head and smiled.

"I will take that as a yes," announced Michael as he sampled the macaroni and cheese.

Feeling a little more like herself, Angelica took a seat at the nook and opened the letter. She had been waiting for a report from Dress Smart. Dress Smart was a branch of LAS focused on acquiring interview attire for needy women.

"You are mighty quiet over there," Angelica said as she began to read the contents of the envelope.

"You stay over there little lady," Michael joked.

About a third of the way into the letter Angelica jumped up from her seat and began to scream. "Oh my gosh! Oh my gosh!"

"What?" exclaimed Michael as he dropped his spoon and turned to see what was going on.

"Why am I being punished like this?" she cried as she held the letter so tightly that it was now a crumbled ball.

Rushing to her side, Michael took the letter from Angelica who laid her head on the counter and cried.

"Let me see," Michael insisted.

"Dear Mrs. Harrison:

Since the inception of Lillie Ann Sisters Inc., it has been our goal to foster healthy and supportive relationships with the community by offering a variety of services from upstanding women of the area. We are writing to inform you the LAS Board of Directors has chosen Karen Jameson as President. Outlined in our bylaws is a provision that allows for special elections by the Board in the case of an emergency vacancy. As you know our dear sister Louise had to step down due to health concerns, and in her absence, you have performed unlike any other sister of LAS could have with such short notice. Our decision to select Karen Jameson was not easy but, as you know, we are due to attend several events in the coming months that require solid leadership in place.

It is the Board's hope that you will consider running in the election next year.
All the best,
LAS Board of Directors"

After the shock of the letter, all Angelica wanted to do was lay down in bed with hopes that once she woke up the next day, all of her trouble would disappear. Little by little, everything was slipping out of Angelica's control.

Eleven

Angelica closed the trunk with her elbow as she tried to juggle the two brown paper bags filled with groceries. It was early, Angelica said to herself as she headed to her front door.

"I hate mornings," she grumbled as she jingled her keys in her hand and tried to put them in the door.

"Let me help you with that," Angelica heard a familiar voice say, causing her to jump. Angelica knew Evelyn's voice anywhere.

Before she could even turn around, Angelica took a deep breath and prepared for the worst. Evelyn reached for a bag and leaned against the open screen door.

"Evelyn, what are you doing here so early in the morning?" Angelica asked as she tried not to make eye contact with her sister.

"Oh, I was just in the neighborhood," Evelyn lied.

Once Angelica unlocked the door, she set her bag down and reached for the bag her sister was holding.

"I'll bring it in," Evelyn said as she forced herself past her sister.

"Wonderful," Angelica whispered, closing the door and leaning against it.

It had become obvious to everyone that Angelica was steering clear of her sister, and for good reason. With all the allegations, rumors and backlash swirling around the family and the community, Angelica didn't want to be involved any more than she had to.

By the time Angelica arrived in the kitchen, Evelyn was already unloading the groceries and putting them in the wrong places.

"Ev, why don't you have a seat? Do you want some tea?" Angelica asked as she grabbed a bag of sugar from her sister's hand.

"No, I don't want any tea," she snapped, looking at Angelica like she was crazy. "Why are you putting the sugar there?"

"Because that's where we keep it, Ev," Angelica said and calmly changed the subject. "To what do I owe this visit?"

"We need to talk about…about…about all of this."

Angelica knew why her sister was there but was hoping it had all blown over. Kenneth had been dead for several months and still there were whispers and stares that told Evelyn and Angelica they weren't in the clear just yet.

"All of what?" Angelica asked curiously.

"Cut the mess, Angelica. If one of us is guilty of anything—and I don't think we are—then both of us are. So instead of thinking everything is okay, we need to come up with a game plan," Evelyn said quickly.

Angelica hadn't even thought of having to come up with a "game plan" because in her mind the sisters hadn't done anything *that* bad.

"Ev, listen, all of this will blow over once Christie has a chance to cool off. She's still mourning. We all are."

For someone who was in the middle of a pretty big accusation, Evelyn thought Angelica was sure acting calm and aloof.

"You do remember what we both decided to do, right?" Evelyn asked, trying to snap her sister out of her fantasy daydream.

Angelica just shook her head and continued putting away groceries. For the first time, Evelyn was convinced her sister was in denial.

"Angelica, listen to me," Evelyn said as she stood up and placed her hands on her sister's shoulders, turning her around so they faced one another.

"Evelyn, what's your—" Angelica started before being cut off by Evelyn.

"We *both* decided to do this. Both of us. We knew Christie was the beneficiary on his life insurance policy. So, yeah, we might have decided to do things a little bit differently before Kenneth's death. It didn't hurt anyone," Evelyn said as she loosened her grip, "right?"

Angelica searched her sister's face and didn't have a reply. She had tried her best to block out thoughts of their earlier discussions and most importantly what they'd agreed to do before their brother's death.

"I...I don't know..." Angelica replied as she dropped onto a chair.

Silence filled the room like an unwanted guest and it wasn't until Evelyn cleared her throat and started to speak that it left.

"I just remember thinking at the time it was the right thing to do. I mean, between the two of us, we were spending so much time at that hospital and so much time away from home. And I know in my heart, had we asked Kenneth for the money, he would've given it to us. But..."

"But we didn't..." Angelica said with a deep breath.

In an instant, just as their emotions began to peek out, Evelyn's attitude changed.

"We did nothing wrong, Angelica. Christie is forgetting everything we did for her father, everything we sacrificed and she's doing this? All of this? And for what? For attention? For the money? For what?"

"I just can't believe that after everything we've done and been through, this ungrateful brat has the nerve to accuse us—her own aunts—for something like this."

The sisters sat quietly fuming as Angelica's words lingered in the room. They wanted this to all be over because the attention wasn't the kind they liked. People were starting to whisper that they were thieves, liars and manipulators and neither of the sisters were handling it well.

"So what are we going to do?" Angelica asked quietly when she couldn't take the silence any more. As she'd learned since her brother's death, silence was not her friend. Far too often, it left her with nothing more than her thoughts and her tears. In her mind, she had taken Kenneth's death far harder than Evelyn. He was her rock and although he was her baby brother, she had looked up to him. Since his death, Angelica had started to do whatever she could to avoid thinking about him being gone and about the accusations hanging over her and Evelyn's heads.

"We're going to fight this!" Evelyn yelled so loud it snapped Angelica out of her daydream.

"Fight it? Why? Don't you think we should just—"

"Angelica, get a backbone. Think about it. We were the ones who had the most contact with Kenneth before his death. We took care of him. We were with him when he passed away. We knew what he wanted."

"But what he wanted wasn't exactly what we did. If we're going to fight this we need to have a better alibi than what you just said."

Finally, the truth was setting in and Angelica was able to see this wasn't going anywhere. Looking at her sister, Evelyn softened up a little bit.

"We knew that Kenneth wanted Christie to be the beneficiary on everything, right? We didn't mess with anything other than the bank account and that was because, well, things changed at the last minute. We didn't expect it to go the way it did with Kenneth, so we improvised."

Angelica took a deep breath, "Did we do the right thing?"

Evelyn immediately returned to her aggressive self and snapped back, "We did the right thing for us. If you don't think so then maybe you should turn yourself in to the police, fork over your possessions and my salon, then sit back and watch Christie take everything because of a small misunderstanding. She knows we wouldn't steal from her father. Now we just have to prove it to the detectives."

"When is the last time you saw Christie?" Angelica asked. "She tried calling a few times but I just haven't been in much of a talkative mood lately. And she came by the house the day before the funeral threatening Michael and I. If it hadn't been for Junior and the neighbors being out there, there's no telling what might've happened."

"Oh my goodness."

"Out in my front yard causing a scene and being ignorant for no reason at all. I had to call the police. She left before they got here but I just had to let her know I was not playing with her. She's taking this way too far. I didn't tell you because I didn't want to upset you before the funeral."

"Deborah came by the salon last week and told me Christie had been calling her at work too just a few days ago," Evelyn said, shaking her head. "This brat is something else. Why won't she just leave all of this alone? It's not as if Kenneth didn't leave her everything else. And Deborah? Don't even get me started on her."

Angelica chuckled a bit. Neither of the sisters had ever really cared too much for their brother's fiancée but publicly they put up a front that she was one of them. Privately, though, they roasted her like a pig on an open flame.

"She has some nerve to even stick her nose into things that no longer concern her. I think she was with Kenneth for his money anyway. I don't trust her at all. Never have," Evelyn said.

For once, the sisters agreed on something.

Evelyn wasn't sure if it was because her brother's time with her had been cut short due to his relationship with Deborah, but something about Deborah had never sat well with her.

"She seems like an opportunistic woman to me. I mean, who knows if Kenneth was the only one she was dating. She probably forced him to propose," Evelyn said evilly.

The sisters laughed in unison, only stopping when Junior slowly entered the room.

The sisters' eyes darted to one another as they wondered how long he had been standing there.

"Hey Junior," Evelyn said as she carefully eyed her nephew.

Angelica turned her back and wiped away imaginary crumbs as Junior went into the kitchen cabinet and took his usual chips and salsa down for a snack.

"What are y'all in here talking about?" Junior asked curiously.

He knew he had walked into something, but he wasn't sure what. His Aunt Evelyn was always gossiping about someone and his mother always seemed to go along with it.

"Oh nothing, just shooting the breeze," Evelyn said with a mischievous grin.

"Sounded like more than nothing to me," Junior said as he shrugged his shoulders and headed back to the guest room just as Evelyn's cell phone began to ring.

Her eyes widened as she answered the phone slowly. "Hey Deborah, Angelica and I were just sitting here talking about you....of course all good... how are you? Really? When? I'll definitely be by to see you a little later today. Alright, girl. Take care! Bye," Evelyn said in a phony high-pitched tone. She even surprised herself at how well she could act as if she liked Deborah when she hated her very existence.

When Evelyn hung up, she grimaced. "Christie came by the funeral home yesterday asking questions about Kenneth's death certificate and a few other things."

Angelica calmly stated, "This is why we're going to have to fight."

Twelve

"Junior?" Christie said with a grin on her face. Although the two had always been close, she was still getting used to having him call her on a regular basis. It felt good to have *some* family around when she needed them the most. And though Junior was in a sticky situation with his mother being in the middle of the big drama, Christie didn't hold that against him. He was her favorite cousin and she loved him.

"Hey, Chris," Junior replied, sounding a little off.

"How are you? Is everything okay?" Christie asked as she took a seat in an oversized leather chair.

Life had been a constant battle for Christie since her father's death and she wondered when it would start to seem like less of a fight and more joyful. She had been going back and forth with her aunts about her father's bank account and in the midst of it she was packing up all of her father's belongings in his home. Christie hated having to leave Anthony in Indianapolis to come back to Chicago, but flying back and forth became a norm until she had taken care of everything at her father's house.

"I'm…I'm okay. How are you?" Junior asked with concern in his voice.

"I've been better. I'm just at my dad's house packing things up."

She hadn't spoken much about what she was going to do with her father's home but as she and Anthony had decided, the best thing to do was to pack away Kenneth's personal belongings and rent out the house. This way, they figured, the home would still belong to them should they ever be in a position to move back to Chicago.

"Seems like all I'm doing lately is packing."

Junior listened to his cousin go on for a few moments about what she was going through before he interrupted.

"Have you found out more about the situation between you, my mom and Aunt Evelyn? I'm sure you have, but no one will tell me anything."

Christie sat back and reflected on her cousin's question. Part of her wanted to tell the world while the other part was embarrassed her family was even in this situation.

"What do you mean?" Christie asked, buying herself some time.

"I mean, I know you've found out more since the last time we spoke and I want to know what's going on. I know they aren't going to tell me but I kind of hoped you would."

There was no delicate way to say what Christie needed to say. No way to dress up the ugly facts. She didn't know how Junior would take it so she just blurted it out.

"I have pretty solid proof that your mom and Aunt Evelyn stole the money from my father's account while he lay dying in the hospital."

There was a long pause on the phone as Christie imagined Junior doing his best to understand what his favorite cousin was telling him about his mother and aunt. He knew from their last conversation that she'd had her suspicions, but he was hoping they were wrong. Christie knew that Junior and Angelica had never had the best of relationships, but who wanted to hear that their mother was a thief?

"And…you're sure? You have proof?" Junior mumbled, barely loud enough for Christie to make out what he was saying.

Christie thought to herself, even with all the evidence and all the gut feelings she had, *was* she sure? Was she certain and without a doubt that her aunts had stolen from her father?

Before she could answer, her mind wandered back to the day when Junior called to tell her he was leaving home, more than ten years earlier.

"What are you talking about, Junior?" Christie asked as she pushed her glasses on top of her head and listened intently. She had always known that her cousin and aunt had a volatile relationship, but she never thought it would lead to him moving out.

"I'm leaving home, Chris. I can't stand it here with her…or him. Nothing I do is ever right. Nothing I say is ever right. It's like they want me to live up to something but they don't want to give me the room to even get there. I'm just sick of it."

Christie was in her last year of college at the time and stressed to the max but knew she needed to make time for Junior.

Growing up, the two had always been close and although Christie was a few years older, they had essentially grown up together.

"Junior, are you sure this is what you want to do? Your parents do a lot for you right now. Have you saved up?" Christie asked gently. She could tell Junior was in a sensitive state and the last thing she wanted to do was upset him anymore. Still, she didn't want to sugarcoat the facts.

"I haven't done any of that, Chris. I just can't take it. Can I come and stay with you for a few weeks until I get on my feet?" Junior asked.

Before she could object she heard herself agree. So there they were, favorite cousins living under the same roof for three weeks while Junior plotted his next move. During that time, they grew closer and deepened their friendship. Junior helped Christie with the housework while Christie slaved at school all day. She had to admit she liked his company and was sad when he left. He hadn't said where he was going or why, but Christie figured he had found a job.

"Chris, are you there?" Junior shouted, as Christie shook herself out of her reminiscing.

"Yeah, I'm here."

"I asked you if you were sure. How do you know?"

Christie was done protecting a family that wasn't trying to protect her.

"Yes, I'm sure, Junior. I've asked questions. I've gotten facts. I know without any doubt that they did the unthinkable. They stole from my dad while he lay dying in the hospital. Why do you ask? What have you heard?"

Junior let the silence dance around them.

"I was at my mom's house and overheard her and Aunt Evelyn talking."

Christie pulled the phone closer as she replied, "What did you hear?"

Junior seemed guarded but told his cousin everything he could. "I don't know what all I heard, I just know they were going on and on about you suing them and about not doing anything *that* bad. I knew something was wrong because even Aunt Evelyn seemed shaken by the discussion."

Christie grinned but a part of her heart hurt. She was sure what she knew was true but to hear it from Junior hurt.

"What else did you hear? Did they—?" Christie said as she heard a knock on the door.

"Junior, let me call you back. I think this is the neighbor," Christie said as she peered out the peephole.

Christie opened the door and stared at the next-door neighbor, Julius Thompson, her father had often called "Mr. Grumps." Mr. Thompson stood about 5'10", had neat dreadlocks that dangled over his shoulders and wore a grey sweater and creased jeans. Mr. Thompson had a solemn look on his face as Christie forced a smile on hers.

"Can I help you?"

"Hi, are you Christie?"

"Yes." She had learned not to expect a warm welcome from anyone so she had stopped being as outgoing as she once had been.

"I'm Julius Thompson. I live…well, I lived across the street from your father," he said as he pointed to the house with a well-manicured lawn.

She wasn't sure if Mr. Thompson was there to pay his respects or to tell her something. He looked like it was the latter, so Christie cleared her throat and softened her tone, "Is everything okay?"

Mr. Thompson nodded, but his face said something *wasn't* okay.

"I wanted to check if they'd had any updates on the burglary that occurred while your father was in the hospital. Did they find any leads? Did they make any arrests?"

Christie opened the door a little bit more. She had been told about a burglary that occurred while her father was hospitalized but with everything else going on she hadn't checked on the status of it.

"The police just told me that they were looking into things. I haven't heard much more," Christie said as she laid her head on the door. So much had happened in a short span of time that Christie found it hard to keep up with it all.

"I promise once we figure everything out, I'll let you know."

"I was the one who called the police so please do. All I know is that I saw people coming in and out with TVs, stereos, tools and expensive things. I thought it was your family but when the police came and asked me what I'd seen, they told me it was a robbery. Your father was such a nice man. It's a shame that all of this had to happen to him at once."

Christie nodded her head and closed her eyes.

"You tell me if you need anything...anything at all." Mr. Thompson said as he backed up and headed towards his own front door.

Christie closed the door and slammed her back against it as she slid down to the floor. It was becoming harder and harder to keep things from falling apart but as things would start to come together, she would finally see just how much it all depended on her keeping her composure in order for it to make sense.

Thirteen

"This is Christie," she said as she answered her phone while watching the person in front of her order a latte.

"Hey, stranger," Janice said in a tone that was more cautious than excited.

Janice and Christie hadn't spoken since their meeting at the news station. Janice had promised to pull a few favors and find out what she could about the mystery of Christie's father's finances.

"Hey there!" Christie said, forcing a smile on her face. She eyed the menu like she had never been in Starbucks before and didn't know what to order as she tried to make up her mind.

"How have you been? I mean...*really*?" Janice asked, not missing a beat.

Christie took a second to respond because she knew if she lied, Janice would know.

"I've been doing better. Really."

And it was true. The weeks were rolling by and while she didn't feel one step closer to figuring everything out about her father's finances and the missing money, she felt like she was starting to accept her new reality. Accepting things didn't make it easier, just tolerable.

"Good. I didn't know if I was going to have to come over and force feed you a few martinis," Janice joked.

Christie chuckled and shook her head. Janice always knew the right tone to use to get a smile out of her.

"Can I help you?" asked a pimple-faced, teenage boy as Christie made her way to the front of the line.

"Um…can I have a…" Christie sighed as she tapped her chin.

It wasn't that she didn't know what she wanted, it was that she hated that she did. All her life, Christie had been the predictable one. The one who always ordered chicken fingers, fries and pink lemonade. The one who always blasted Anita Baker's music. She was safe and she knew it.

"Let me have a Venti Caramel Macchiato with soy milk and no foam."

Even when she tried to step outside her norm, she frightened herself enough to retreat to the regular way of doing things.

Once she'd paid and received her drink order, Christie sat outside at one of the bistro tables.

"When are you ever going to try something new at Starbucks, Christie? For as long as I've know you, you've *always* ordered the same thing. You know they do serve things other than Caramel Macchiato, right?" Janice joked.

"Oh hush," Christie said as she sat back in the metal chair and crossed her legs.

"How have things been? Are they kind of returning to normal?" Janice asked curiously.

Janice and Christie's relationship was such that even though they didn't talk every day they still had this undeniable bond and connection that couldn't be broken. When they had worked at the same news station, they could go days without seeing or speaking to each other and their weekly Girls' Night Out consisting of drinks, appetizers and people watching would be filled with conversation.

"I mean, it's never going to be normal as I knew it before my father died and, I guess, that's what I'm coming to accept. But my family has been nothing but confusing. I can't get either of my aunts on the phone and they're ducking and dodging me like I'm the police," Christie replied as she finally took a sip of her warm drink.

"My cousin called the other day to tell me about something he'd overheard from my aunt and his mother but since then I haven't even been able to get in touch with *him*. It's getting frustrating."

"Well, Christmas is coming early for you."

"Oh Lord, what now?"

"I pulled a few strings and used some of my favors from some pretty prominent people in Chicago. And, well, I found some things out. That's really why I called you," Janice said.

Suddenly Christie's heart was racing faster than she'd ever felt it race. It was as if someone was holding the key to her sanity and all she had to do was listen closely enough.

"Talk to me," she replied.

"I have a friend named Bobby Washington, who is a private investigator. I've known him for well over twenty years and he's one of the most straight-forward guys I've ever met. He owes me big-time for landing him a high-profile gig about fifteen years ago that helped jump start his business. I called him and told him all about your situation and he agreed to try to dig around to see what he could find."

Christie's eyes began to water. Until then it had felt like she was digging a hole in sand all by herself. Even this small glimmer of light made Christie hopeful.

"Okay," she said, signaling Janice to continue.

"First, the bank manager, Sara Frederick, has a good chunk of information that we'll need. Right now, Bobby doesn't have it all but what he did get is going to be helpful."

As soon Christie heard the name Sara Frederick, her ears perked up. She knew the name well from the day following her father's death when she'd phoned the bank to put a hold on his account. Everything else about that day was a blur, from what Christie did when she woke up, to the people she spoke with throughout the day, but she remembered Sara Frederick.

Sara had been the voice on the other end of the line informing her that her father only had $1,100 in his account at his time of death. Sara Frederick was the stranger who had opened the door to all the questions that lay ahead of Christie.

"I've spoken with her once," Christie sighed. "The day I found out about all of this."

Janice was in her own world as she rattled off the rest of the information, "Bobby says that according to his sources, the money from your father's account was wired to some secret account set up in New York. Whoever was wiring this money set the account up so securely that even Bobby is having a hard time peeling back the layers. But he's on it."

"New York? My father hasn't lived in New York in years. He was born there but they moved to Chicago when he was a teenager. Do you think someone other than my family could be behind this?"

It was the first time Christie doubted the very thing that she had been so sure about. Had her aunts been victims in this too? Was this all one big misunderstanding? Had she jumped the gun?

"I wish I knew more to tell you right now, kid. Until we find out whose account that money was wired to, we're all pulling straws and guessing."

Christie picked up her drink and held it to her mouth. She had so much she wanted to say but so little that she actually could. It was very bizarre to her.

"Christie, how much money was stolen? I don't think you've ever said," Janice asked with little hesitation.

In fact, outside of her husband, Christie hadn't spoken about the amount stolen from her father to anyone. She wasn't sure if it was because she couldn't bear to say the amount for fear that it would anger her all over again, or if it was because she didn't care about the amount and was more concerned about the principle of it all. Her entire life her father had instilled responsibility in her, especially when it came to finances. They would make weekly trips to the bank together where he taught her how to fill out deposit slips, make balance inquiries, write checks and even open her first savings account which Christie kept throughout her college years. She knew how much saving meant to her father and knowing that on a selfish whim someone had taken it away from him infuriated her.

"It was everything my father had saved in his life, $1.5 million. Everything he had ever put aside for me was stolen. For as long as I can remember, my father had me listed as the beneficiary on all of his accounts, all of his policies and properties so I know my father would not have only had $1,100 in his main account," Christie rambled. "It's just impossible and I know I'm not crazy."

Janice was quiet for a few seconds, "Well, now you know for certain that you're not crazy, Christie. Someone *did* steal money from your father. Now, we've just got to figure out who did it. One more thing, your aunt…I think her name is Angelica? She's married, correct?"

"Yes, to a man named Michael Harrison. I've been trying to get all of them on the phone and it's been virtually impossible."

"Okay." Janice replied, sounding as if she was jotting down notes.

"Why? What's going on?"

"Bobby says there were some sort of financial problems going on with Angelica and her husband. I'm not sure of the specifics, but up until a few months ago their house was close to being foreclosed, their cars nearly repossessed and they owed a lot of money to banks across Chicago. I don't know if it's connected to your father's disappearing money but it's worth Bobby looking into."

Christie's mouth was hanging open. Her aunt broke? Her aunt who loved to flash and brag about how much more she had than everyone else? Christie couldn't believe the words now dancing in her head. Something wasn't making sense.

"I just…I'm flabbergasted, Janice. I leave Chicago tomorrow morning, let's get together."

"Well, let it all sink in and give me a call tomorrow so we can do drinks. I think we're definitely due a round or two of martinis. Call me if you need anything," Janice said quickly.

"Janice," Christie said softly before Janice could hang up, "thank you."

"Anything for you kid. Don't stress too much and just know that every truth, *and* every lie, is going to be revealed. Believe me," Janice said in a comforting tone.

When Christie hung up she had no desire to finish her Caramel Macchiato. Her eyes explored the beautiful scenery. The sun was shining fiercely, people were buzzing in and around the coffee shop and Christie's mind was swirling.

Now we just have to figure out who did it, Christie mumbled to herself as she punched numbers into her cell phone and waited for Anthony to pick up to relay the new information.

Fourteen

Smoke lined the edges of the lounge, dancing around the people in the room.

"Where'd you hear about this place?" Christie asked Janice as she looked around the dark room and forced a grin.

Janice chuckled as she found a booth and took a seat.

"We did a report on it a few months ago and, believe it or not, they have some of the best food and drinks here," Janice replied as she waved a waitress over.

Christie was far from a prude, but since the two of them usually met at upscale restaurants this was definitely different.

"If you say so."

"I do," Janice smirked, as the waitress appeared with two tattered menus.

"What can I start you two off with to drink?" the red-headed, green-eyed woman asked politely. She was wearing all black, with black nail polish as well.

"I'll just take water with lemon, please," Christie said as she fidgeted with her menu.

"Give us two appletinis, honey. Tell the bartender not to be stingy with the spirits, either," Janice joked and winked.

Christie was relieved to be able to unwind with her friend.

"How's Anthony doing? I'm surprised he hasn't talked you into having a baby yet," Janice blurted.

Christie turned her face up at the thought. It wasn't that she didn't want children; she just saw herself and Anthony as still being children themselves. But it was true, Anthony had been making it crystal clear as time went on that his desire for children was growing. Still, with her father's death, Christie had been able to keep her husband at bay when it came to discussing the topic.

"I keep telling you, we're not ready for children yet. Shoot, I can barely decide if I want cereal or eggs for breakfast. I can't even think about having a child right now."

Janice shook her head as the server delivered their drinks, and immediately began sipping hers.

Christie just stared at hers. Maybe it was everything on her mind or maybe it was the unfamiliar setting, but she wasn't in a drinking mood.

"Anthony's fine, though," Christie finally answered, taking a sip of her water.

"Do you two know what you'd like to order?" the waitress asked as she placed one hand on her hip and looked down at the girlfriends.

"Let me order for you…I know exactly what you'll like," Janice said as she took the menu away from Christie.

"Give us two jumbo turkey burgers with extra lettuce, tomato and onions and sweet potato fries, please."

It sounded delicious, Christie thought to herself as the waitress sauntered away and placed their orders with the cook.

"How have you been, Janice? What's new with you?"

Janice took a long sip from her appletini, sat back in the booth and exhaled.

"Well, besides the fact that Channel 6 is kicking our butt in ratings?"

Christie's mouth dropped. Janice's ratings had never fallen below their competitor, Channel 6. Known for their boring anchors and even more boring stories, Channel 6 had always come in a few points behind KTL Indianapolis. Hearing they were ahead was shocking.

"What? How?" Christie asked as her eyes widened. For the moment, she forgot about her personal stresses and she tuned into what was going on with her friend.

Music was blaring around them and people were bustling in and out of the lounge but Christie's attention was entirely on Janice. She was a little *too* laid back for Christie's comfort. The Janice she knew would be flipping tables and bodies over to figure out who and what had caused the shift.

"It's a long story, Christie. Very long," Janice said as she dropped her head and a grin spread across her face.

Now Christie knew something was up. Janice? Laughing about coming in behind Channel 6? Something must be up.

"Talk to me."

"A few months ago, I heard rumors KTL was looking to hire a newer, younger anchor."

Christie almost lost her balance in the booth. Janice couldn't be saying what she thought she was saying. KTL Indianapolis trying to replace Janice? She was practically the face of the city.

"So, you know me, I did some digging and I got to the bottom of things. I approached the board of directors and gave them a choice. They could either keep me on and give me a raise, or they could replace me but lose me to Channel 6."

Christie's eyes widened as if she was reading a suspenseful novel. She leaned forward and placed her elbows on the table as she continued listening.

"So they chose to replace me, effective January first."

Christie couldn't believe everything she was hearing. Janice had been the face of KTL for decades and now she was switching teams? Christie's puzzled face carried more confusion than Janice could handle before speaking up.

"Don't look like that. KTL brought it on themselves, Christie. I've consistently brought them number one ratings and simply because I'm getting older they want to replace me? No. I wasn't having it. I wasn't," Janice said as she stared off into the distance.

A pregnant silence danced around before Christie finally opened her mouth to speak.

"So you'll be working at Channel 6 in the winter? So, wait…why are the ratings low now, if you don't start at Channel 6 for a few months?"

Janice winked mischievously.

"You didn't think I'd make it easy on KTL, did you? I've been prepping Channel 6 with better stories so when I do make my final transition it will be seamless. KTL won't even know what's hit them."

Christie grinned and tried to make sense of everything Janice had told her. The waitress placed their burgers on the tables and topped off Christie's water. Taking one look at her sandwich, Christie felt her appetite turn. The burger *looked* delicious but smelling it was a completely different thing.

Janice, on the other hand, tore into her burger before the waitress had a chance to hand them napkins.

"Aren't you going to eat?" Janice inquired as she slowed down and dabbed the corners of her mouth.

"My stomach doesn't feel right. It might be all this smoke," Christie said as she pushed her burger away. Janice eyed her suspiciously and continued eating her own burger.

Sitting quietly at the table, Christie wasn't sure what had come over her but with her face warm and her stomach in shambles she knew something wasn't right. Over the past few weeks, she had been so stressed that she was no longer eating right or even at all, so she figured it was all catching up to her now. As a wave of nausea hit her, Christie took another brisk sip of her water and exhaled slowly.

She hadn't allowed the stress of her family drama to affect her health up until this point and she wasn't going to let it start now.

"Are you okay?" Janice asked.

Christie nodded and pulled out a compact mirror. She felt funny; she just hoped she didn't *look* funny, too. Peering at her face, she noticed it was definitely a little puffier and the bags under her eyes were bigger. She looked decent, she told herself, but she didn't look top-notch like she normally did. Still, she forced a smile.

"I'm fine," Christie said as an olive-toned man with a dark moustache and dark brown eyes approached their table. He kept his eyes on Christie and she did the same to him. Finally, Janice spoke up.

"Christie, this is Bobby Washington, my friend who's a private investigator. Remember? I told you about him."

Christie breathed a sigh of relief and relaxed in her seat before extending her hand. "Mr. Washington, it's a pleasure."

"Same here," Bobby said confidently as he shook her hand firmly and took a seat at the table.

"Bobby met us so he can give you more information that's surfaced about the money," Janice explained as she nodded her head towards Bobby.

"Christie, first, I want you to know I'm qualified in what I do. I've been working as a private investigator for over twenty years. In that time, I've had a chance to handle everything from family issues -kind of like yours- to court-related issues that needed investigation. So I want you to know I take your case seriously."

Christie was impressed. She knew Janice only dealt with the best, but Bobby seemed to be the real deal.

"I'm still trying to uncover the details about this secret account that the money was initially wired to in New York. Whoever set the account up did a really good job of making it hard to link it back to them. Still, the biggest thing we know is that someone *was* stealing from your father. But whether we can say for certain right now that it was one of your aunts…I don't think so."

"Do you think it's possible it was someone else and all of this is just one big misunderstanding?" Christie asked, wanting to believe the fantasy she had just said aloud.

Janice tilted her head to the side sympathetically and Bobby took a deep breath before replying.

"The fact that we found some financial issues going on with your Aunt Angelica makes me really suspicious. They were on the verge of losing everything and in a matter of months that changed. I'm not saying she's guilty, but I'm also not saying she's in the clear either," Bobby said with a shrug.

Christie nodded. Sometimes, she rationed to herself, it's easier for others to tell us what we know but wish we didn't.

"I understand," she said quietly.

Janice didn't miss a beat and jumped in with her comforting tone that always picked Christie up.

"Christie, I think you should definitely look into hiring Bobby and an attorney. Bobby's done about as much as he can do for free, as a favor to me, but for him to dig deeper you're going to have to hire him. I think having an attorney at this point is almost necessary. There's no telling what you're going to walk into once all these doors start being unlocked and it's better to be prepared."

Christie bit her bottom lip. "Am I really going to have to sue my *family* for my father's money? How do I even explain that to people and…" she started to ramble.

Normally Janice would jump in and comfort her but this time it was Bobby.

"I have a friend who is a lawyer and has handled cases just like yours for years. You can let her firm worry about all those things you're stressing about right now," Bobby said kindly.

Christie's mind was swirling and before she knew it, she had agreed to hire Bobby and to contact the lawyer. As she gathered up her things, Janice stopped her.

"You didn't even touch your appletini, Christie. I told you they're delicious."

Christie smiled and glanced over her shoulder at her friend.

"My appetite is beyond spoiled, Janice, maybe another time."

And just like that, the layers began to peel back.

Fifteen

Christie peered at herself in the bathroom mirror. She couldn't even explain why she was up at such an ungodly hour. Glancing at the clock on the wall, Christie took a deep breath.

"3:30 in the morning, Christie?" she said to herself as she glanced back at the mirror.

Anthony was snoring loudly and Christie had too much on her mind to just lay there and listen to it. She was fine when the sun was up, but as soon as it was replaced by the moon, Christie's ability to keep it all together disappeared.

I have to go to bed, she thought as she stared at her face, which was showing its own signs of stress with budding pimples and excessive oil. Christie ran her fingers over a small pimple and frowned. She didn't have the perfect skin seen on models or actresses, but Christie had always prided herself on having clear skin. Lately, though, her skin and her body hadn't felt like her own. In addition to either not being hungry at all or being nauseous, Christie had now begun to feel the weight of her father's death affecting her sleep patterns.

Heading to her home office, Christie sat down and moved the mouse around a few times until the computer screen lit up.

"When all else fails, scour the internet, right?" Christie said out loud.

It seemed like the more she wanted to distance herself from the foolishness happening with her family, the more she kept pulling herself back into the middle of it.

She scrolled the mouse over the Internet Explorer icon and clicked on it quickly. The screen immediately went to the Google homepage. Christie hesitated before typing in the words that had been jumbled in her brain for the past week—Tyson Hospice. Chicago. Illinois—and hit Enter.

Instantly results began to flood her computer screen. Christie clicked on the first link that led to the company's home page.

For almost a month Christie had replayed a conversation she'd had with her Aunt Angelica while her father was in the hospital. The conversation hadn't seemed out of the ordinary when it happened but as time went on Christie couldn't ignore it.

"Christie, do you have a minute?" Aunt Angelica asked as she stuck her head into Kenneth's hospital room.

"Um…sure, what's up?"

"I know you just got here and it's probably a lot to take in, but your Aunt Evelyn and I have been on top of the doctors to figure out what the next steps are for your father," Angelica said softly.

Christie tried to remain calm. She wasn't sure why the doctor hadn't shared any news with her but, she rationalized, her living out of town probably made it easier to communicate with her aunts.

"We're looking at checking your father into a hospice center called Tyson Hospice. It's supposed to be the best one in the area though I know he'll fight going there. He has some sort of grudge with the owner's son—I think they went to school together or something. But it's best for him," Angelica said with a small smile.

Part of Christie felt relieved. They were talking about releasing her father and, furthermore, about him living.

"Is he going to get better there? Isn't hospice where people go when they're dying?"

"The hospice is the best place for your father right now. The doctors say he needs to stay here but Angelica and I want…I mean, we need…him to go to Tyson's. It's the only way he has a shot at getting better."

"Okay, whatever we need to do to get him better."

Angelica took Christie's hand, *"He's really happy you're here. We all are. It's been rough on all of us. Your dad being sick, I mean."*

Christie was trying to figure out why something felt forced, almost planned, about her aunt's speech.

"Yeah, it's been a lot."

Angelica looked like tears were forming in her eyes. "You know, I never thought Evelyn and I would be the ones taking care of Kenneth. He's the baby after all. I expected us to get old and have him taking care of us. But plans change, right?"

Christie nodded but didn't reply.

"We thought we were going to lose him at one point, Christie. Thank God, he's still with us. I can't even begin to understand what we'd do if something happened to him. Kenneth dying would just mean—"

Christie removed her hands from her aunt's and waved them in her face playfully.

"Aunt Angelica, he'll be okay. We don't even need to entertain the thought of him dying."

"But Christie, we have to be prepared. If he were to die, you know I would take care of you, right? Through everything, I'd take of anything you need. I'm your aunt and while I might not do everything perfectly, I will make sure you're taken care of."

Christie opened her mouth to reply and was, instead, surprised to see her father's fiancée rounding the corner. Deborah looked cute with her hair brushed back and minimal make-up. She looked like she'd gone for that "I tried but don't want to seem like it" look—and it worked for her.

Angelica immediately shut down and diverted her eyes.

"Hey, y'all," *Deborah said eyeing Angelica closely.*

"Hey," *Christie said,* "Dad's watching television."

More than anything, Christie wanted to get to the bottom of what her aunt was talking about. Something seemed cryptic about her statement and she needed an ounce of clarity.

"Yes, let's all go join him," *Angelica said as she pushed past Christie and Deborah. Christie made a mental note to corner her aunt later to get more details.*

Snapping out of her daydream, Christie swirled the mouse around the tan and purple website filled with pictures of smiling elderly people and pretty fonts. Clicking on the "About" section of the website, she learned Tyson Hospice had opened in 1994 by Harold and Eleanor Tyson. The older couple smiled widely in their portrait, wearing their Sunday-best attire. They looked friendly too, Christie thought.

She wasn't sure what she was looking for or why Tyson Hospice had stuck in her mind, but her mind was leading her.

Christie clicked through a few pictures on the website and found herself smiling. All the people in the photos looked so happy to be at the hospice center. While some people might have figured hospice patients would be gloomy and down, these patients looked ecstatic.

"It looks like a vacation or something," Christie said in disbelief, "and can you believe—" she stopped mid-sentence as she paused on a picture. At least five years old, it showed the owners embracing a woman and a child. Normally, Christie would have overlooked the picture but she thought she'd zeroed in on something fishy.

"What the heck is Deborah doing in the picture with the owners?" she asked herself as she narrowed her eyes and leaned closer to the screen.

There was no denying it, old picture or not, Deborah was somehow affiliated with the same hospice center where her family wanted her father to end up staying.

Christie had a great memory. When they'd first met, Deborah told her she'd retired from the post office and was now working part-time at the funeral home. There was no mention of ever having worked at a hospice center. Christie was intrigued by the mystery before her.

She clicked back to the "About" section and scanned the bio of the owners again. Line by line, Christie searched for something she'd overlooked. Then she saw it—Harold and Eleanor Tyson have one daughter, Deborah Tyson, which was her maiden name prior to being married and later divorced.

Christie opened her email account and drafted an email.

SUBJECT: *Suspicions*

Bobby- Please call me at your earliest convenience tomorrow. I've just stumbled onto something that has me baffled. I think I know why the funeral home was giving me a hard time…or maybe I've figured out a motive for the lies. There's a place called Tyson Hospice in Chicago that may be linked. I don't know.

Please call.

Thanks, Christie

Now the pieces of the puzzle were becoming much more confusing.

Christie heard the phone ringing, but shrugged it off. A few minutes later it rang again. After finally falling asleep at seven that morning, Christie was tired. Still, she knew the phone ringing urgently meant she had to answer it.

"Hello?" she said groggily.

"Christie, it's Bobby. I just got your email. We need to talk."

Christie sat up in her bed, leaned against the headboard and tried to get her bearings together.

"I'm listening."

Bobby seemed like he was nearly whispering, which alarmed Christie.

"The funeral home is owned by the Thomason's. David is the principal," Bobby said in a hushed tone. "There was some fishy business going on around the time of your father's death with the funeral home and the mysterious account in New York."

"What?" Christie shouted.

"I don't know if the person who opened this mysterious account in New York was thinking someone was onto them or what, but it looks like money was transferred from that account to the Thomason's business account."

"Could it have been for the funeral? I think we paid like $20,000 for dad's funeral."

"There was well over $100,000 transferred, Christie. I highly doubt it was for the funeral."

Christie was trying to catch her breath. Everything was being thrown at her so quickly.

"This is one of the strangest cases I've ever seen," Bobby said, sounding a bit flabbergasted.

"It looks now like someone at that funeral home is linked to whoever stole your father's money. Right now I can't say for certain who it is, but just know that I'm on the case."

Words jumbled in her mind, but she couldn't seem to get anything out.

"Christie," Bobby said after a few seconds, "Are you there?"

"I'm here," she said softly. "I'm just more confused than ever and every time I think something's piecing together, it turns out to be another twist and turn. I'm just tired."

Bobby's tone turned sympathetic. "Be patient, Christie. Right now we have the benefit of things falling into our lap. We're going to get to the bottom of everything. Now, about the email you sent me concerning Tyson Hospice. What's going on there?"

Christie was so consumed with the information Bobby had shared with her that she had completely forgotten about Tyson Hospice.

"Something odd is going on there. My Aunt Angelica was talking about putting my father in Tyson Hospice but he passed away before that happened.

Still, I remembered the name and went online to research the place this morning."

"Okay," Bobby replied, sounding like he was taking notes.

"When I looked through their website I noticed my father's fiancée, Deborah Matthews, in a photo hugging the owners. I checked a little bit more and found out she's their daughter. I thought it was strange that she would be tied in with the funeral home *and* the hospice center yet no one ever mentioned the link," Christie said, getting upset.

"Deborah Matthews, you said?" Bobby asked.

"Yes."

"And Tyson Hospice is in Chicago, correct?"

"Yes. My aunt made a comment that my father wouldn't be excited about going to Tyson Hospice because he had an issue with the owner's son, but according to the website they didn't have a son, just a daughter, Deborah."

"Interesting," Bobby said, "Very, very interesting."

Christie took a deep breath, reassured that she wasn't losing her mind.

"Give me a few days, Christie. I'm on assignment now for another client but I wanted to make sure I called and at least checked in with you."

"Thanks, Bobby," Christie said as she pulled the covers back and prepared to get up from the bed.

"No problem. Don't you for one second think I'm not on this. It might take a while but we're going to crack it."

Christie smiled, bid Bobby goodbye, hung up and headed downstairs to the kitchen. On her way down, she gripped the rail as she felt herself getting dizzy. She tripped and her feet stumbled down the steps before safely making her way down. Rounding the corner to the kitchen, Christie leaned on the counter and took deep breaths. She felt strange. Anthony had gone for his morning run, she remembered, and probably wouldn't be back for another hour. After mustering the strength to open the fridge Christie's legs gave way just as everything went black.

Christie had passed out.

Sixteen

"You realize that I hate doctor's offices, right?" Christie whined as Anthony turned into the parking lot.

"And I hate finding my wife passed out on the kitchen floor. I guess we both have things we hate, huh?" Anthony said with a slight smirk.

After returning from his morning run to find Christie sprawled on the kitchen floor passed out cold, Anthony immediately panicked.

"Baby, please don't die. Please be okay," Anthony cried as he picked his wife up and carried her to the couch. As he dialed 911, Anthony heard Christie moan.

"What's going on?" she asked as she tried to prop herself up on her elbows. The room was spinning and she couldn't remember how she'd ended up on the couch.

"Baby…" Anthony said with relief as he entered the room and stared at his wife.

She looked disheveled but she was alive.

"Why on earth am I lying on the couch?" Christie asked as she tried again to sit up. This time though her body quickly let her know who was in control.

"Whoa," she said weakly as she grabbed her forehead.

Anthony hurried to the couch, sat down beside his wife and reached to rub her shoulders.

"You passed out, Chris."

Christie screwed up her face and tried to understand why the words coming out Anthony's mouth sounded like a foreign language. What did he mean she'd passed out?

"Why? What do you mean?" she asked with her hand still on her forehead.

"I don't know. I came in from my run and you were passed out in the kitchen. You scared me, woman. How do you feel?"

It would've been easy to lie and say she felt great, but Anthony knew her. He knew her lies and her truths; he knew her ways better than she did.

"I feel like someone stole all of my energy and bashed me over the head with a brick," she said as she laid her head back.

"Well, Dr. Silver was able to squeeze us in. Hopefully he can give us some insight into what's going on. You've been acting weird lately," Anthony said as he put the car in park and looked over at his wife.

She was still beautiful to him and every breath she took still mattered more than he could ever explain. But something had been off with her lately and he couldn't put his finger on what it was.

"Weird? Why do you say that? And why is this the first time you've…" Christie said angrily as she lifted her head then quickly put it back down. Lowering her voice, she took a few deep breaths and calmly started her question over.

"Babe, why are you just now telling me that I've been acting weird? I had no idea…" Christie said as she looked to the floor.

Anthony sucked his teeth. He knew Christie too well.

"You've had bad insomnia and you've been putting on weight, babe. I know you notice it. I didn't say anything because, well, I didn't want to upset you any more than all of this other stuff has," he said, motioning with his arms. "The last thing you need to hear from me is that it looks like you've put on a few pounds and have a crazy sleeping schedule."

Christie exhaled as she nodded her head.

"You can lose the weight and get back on a regular sleeping schedule but we need to make sure everything is okay, especially since you passed out this morning."

Anthony patted Christie's hand, got out of the car and headed to open her door.

The sun was shining fiercely, so Christie slid her sunglasses on and reached for Anthony's arm to steady herself as she exited the car.

"I hate doctor's offices," she repeated all the way to the door.

Christie's hatred for doctor's offices ran deep. Way deep. When she was a little girl she'd had an allergic reaction to peanuts that left her in the hospital for a few days. After numerous shots, tests and doctor visits, Christie was able to go back to living a "normal" peanut-free life. Still, the painful shots and the terrible waiting she and her parents had endured stayed with her and settled into a strong dislike of doctor's offices.

"Hi, I'm Anthony Adams and my wife, Christie, has an appointment with Dr. Silver. I just called," Anthony said as he fidgeted with the pen and pad in front of the older receptionist. The woman had skin as chocolate as any Hershey bar and a smile that was comforting as one, too.

"Sure thing. Y'all have been here before, right?" she asked sweetly.

"Yes. He is our primary doctor."

It was a shame that neither of them had stepped foot in Dr. Silver's office in years but still called him their primary physician. Anthony didn't go because he felt like he did a dynamic job of eating healthy and working out on a regular basis. Christie didn't go because she hated doctor's offices.

"Have a seat and we'll be right with you. It shouldn't be too long," the woman replied.

Christie sat in one of the cushiony chairs and wrapped her arms around Anthony's. Something about his presence made everything else irrelevant. Nuzzling her head on his shoulder, Christie closed her eyes. With everything else going on, she hadn't updated Anthony on what Bobby had told her or what she'd found out on her own.

"Babe, I was searching online this morning and found something really interesting..."

Anthony peered over and took a deep breath. "Does this have anything to do with your aunts and the money?" he asked with a raised eyebrow.

Christie sat up and stared at him, "Yes it does. Is that a problem?"

Anthony looked around the nearly empty waiting room and then back at his wife. He didn't want to argue and he definitely wasn't trying to upset her but more than anything he wanted her to focus on his immediate concern—her.

"Christie, for this next hour or so can we please not talk about anything to do with that situation? I think it's the reason you're so stressed out, losing sleep, overeating and probably why you fainted today. So forgive me for not wanting to discuss it right now," Anthony said in a hushed tone.

"Okay, babe, okay," Christie said softly as she fixed her eyes on the television.

Truth be told, Christie was tired of having to think about it all and wished she could temporarily teleport to another less stressful time. Gripping Anthony's hand, Christie squeezed it to let him know she was with him. It was rare when Anthony got upset or frazzled so to see him that way moved Christie.

"Mrs. Adams," a young, petite nurse practitioner called.

Christie and Anthony followed her into the examining room. After she was weighed and had her temperature taken, Christie climbed on the examining table and laid back.

"The doctor will be in with you shortly," the young woman said as she exited the room.

Christie laid her head back on the table and stared at the ceiling. So many thoughts were swirling in her head—so many she didn't want there—she did the only thing she could think to do—close her eyes. Before she knew it, she had dozed off.

"Mrs. Adams…" Dr. Silver said with a wide grin as he looked at a folder and then at her. Anthony was sitting in a chair on the wall.

"Yes. I'm sorry, was I sleep?"

"It's okay. These rooms are cold and I'd fall asleep in them too," the doctor joked as Christie sat up.

"So tell me what's going on today. Your husband called in such a frenzy we thought we were going to have to tell him to take you straight to the ER but then you woke up."

Dr. Silver was an older African-American doctor with speckles of silver in his neatly combed Afro. He had a smile that would make anyone happy and a personality that made patients fall in love with him. It was the main reason Christie and Anthony had chosen him as their primary physician even if they didn't see him regularly.

"I don't know what happened. The last thing I remember was trying to make my way down to the kitchen then I woke up on the couch."

Anthony cleared his throat before butting in with his own comments.

"Dr. Silver, she's leaving a lot out. Her father recently passed and she's having a lot of family issues that I think are contributing to her weight gain, having insomnia and passing out. I think all of this is really taking a toll on her."

Dr. Silver listened intently and made a few notes.

Christie kept her eyes straight on the door in front of her. She felt ashamed of all the things Anthony was saying. It wasn't that she didn't want to acknowledge she was going through things, but to know they had begun affecting her health made her feel weak.

"Well, let's take a look at a few things," Dr. Silver said as he listened to her lungs and poked and prodded her body.

After he finished examining her, he took a seat on the stool and asked Anthony to sit back in the chair as well. "You know, we aren't able to diagnose a lot of things until we run blood tests; those are our greatest tools. I can tell you what I think but without blood test results it's irrelevant. So I'm going to order some tests for this afternoon and we should get the results back within a week. Once we do, we'll call you in to discuss what the tests show," Dr. Silver said as he stood up and went to the sink to wash his hands.

"Dr. Silver," Anthony said calmly, "I know you can't tell us for sure but in your professional opinion what are some of the things it *could* be?"

Christie had wanted to ask the question but was too afraid.

Dr. Silver took a deep breath and dried his hands. "Well, it could be anything from a thyroid issue to pregnancy. There's no way for us to know without tests. With all the symptoms you've given me, though, it sounds like a thyroid issue. Christie is generally in pretty good shape and well-rested. Some of the splotches I see on her face, though, are similar to those that I see on women with early Polycystic Ovarian Syndrome or PCOS. PCOS basically means the woman's hormones are out of whack. It can cause a host of problems like weight gain, increased facial and body hair, irregular cycles and sometimes infertility."

"In…infertility?" Christie said with worry in her voice.

Anthony stroked her hand as he stared at the doctor for reassurance. They had made it clear that they didn't want children now, but they definitely wanted children one day.

"Let's not jump to conclusions. We won't know anything until we get those tests back. Let's worry about things then. For now, go home and get plenty of rest and fluids."

Christie nodded and forced a smile on her face. As much as she hated doctors, she hated leaving a doctor's office with no answer as to what was wrong even more.

"I'm going to write you a prescription for a safe sleep aid. This is non-habit forming but it will help with your insomnia."

"Thanks, Dr. Silver," Anthony said as he stood up and shook the doctor's hand.

"Let's go home and lay down," Anthony grinned towards his wife.

As they walked down the hallway, Christie couldn't help but grab her husband's hand. He had always been super protective of her but today she was more thankful than ever.

"Let's get a bite to eat, then head to the house and take a nap. We can pick your prescription up on the way home," Anthony said opening the door for his wife.

As if on cue, Christie bumped into her Aunt Evelyn. Stumbling backwards, each of them stood wide-eyed, staring at each other as if they'd never seen one another.

"Christie," Evelyn said in a matter-of-fact tone.

Christie didn't reply, just clenched Anthony's hand tighter.

"Well, isn't it *interesting* running into you here?" Evelyn continued as she eyed her niece up and down like a stranger who made her skin crawl.

Christie had been having daydreams about this moment, about what might be said when she ran into Evelyn or Angelica, but right now she was only drawing blanks. Her irrational mind told her to have a few choice words with her aunt while laying hands on her, but Christie knew that would get her nowhere.

"You know, I've thought long and hard about what I'd say if I ever came face-to-face with you," Christie started as she loosened her grip on Anthony's hand.

Evelyn raised an eyebrow and crossed her arms over her chest.

"I don't know what you and Aunt Angelica did or why, but the truth is going to come to light; remember that."

Evelyn opened her mouth to reply but Christie cut her off.

"And you know what's so disgusting? Through everything, my father always told me if anything ever happened to him that I was to make sure I stuck by family. It seems like family was the first to turn on him, though."

Evelyn's jaw dropped as Christie walked past her and headed towards the car. Anthony opened her door, helped her in and then rushed to the driver's side to start the car.

"Wow, Chris," Anthony said under his breath as they made their way out of the parking lot. Christie felt many emotions—empowered, saddened, hopeful and angry—but mostly she felt confused.

Glancing in the side mirror, Christie saw her aunt watch their car pull out into traffic and then walk towards the doctor's office door.

She'd had so much to say but didn't feel like she had gotten anything resolved or any closer to an answer.

"I hate doctor's offices," she said as she shifted in her seat and closed her eyes.

Seventeen

Christie laid her head back on the soft pillow. It was so cold in the house that she wondered if someone had left a door open. Anthony had gone to run errands and made Christie promise not to get up from the bed until he returned. Bored out her mind, Christie flipped through the channels.

"Why is it so cold in here?" Christie asked herself as she pulled the covers up higher. She had more on her mind than cold air and pointless television programs. Running into her Aunt Evelyn outside the doctor's office had definitely shaken her up more than she cared to admit.

Maybe it was the smirk on Evelyn's face or maybe it was her body language. Whatever it was, Christie didn't like it. It was so cold that Christie was transported to a dream where she was in her father's similarly cold hospital room. Her mind began to wander to that pale room and her eyes began to water as she thought back to one of her last trips to see her father.

It was freezing outside. Christie bundled up and headed to the hospital to check on her father. Things weren't looking great for him but, she rationalized, he always pulled through any hard time so why was this any different?

This was her third visit since her father was hospitalized and unlike the first Christie and Evelyn bumped heads immediately. Gone was the suspiciously sweet, outgoing aunt; now Evelyn acted as if Christie's presence was a nuisance. Christie felt so out of place staying at her aunt's house that she had contemplated getting a hotel room, but knew her father would have a fit. She had already rented a car because she didn't want to rely on her Aunt Evelyn to get to and from the hospital. Her father would probably lose his mind if she opted to stay in a hotel. So as always she sucked it up and put a smile on her face. Christie would have preferred to stay with her mother but since Alise and her husband lived about an hour and a half outside of the city that would have been a cumbersome commute to and from the hospital each day.

"It's only temporary," she told herself.

Making her way into her father's room, Christie found a nurse feeding him breakfast and excused her to do the honors herself.

"Hey, Daddy," Christie said as she took her jacket off and slid into the chair beside his bed.

"Hey, baby girl," he replied weakly. Some days he sounded stronger and others it sounded like it took every ounce of his energy to complete a sentence. Whatever was slowly killing her father was also slowly killing Christie's spirit.

"Looks like you have some good breakfast today—eggs, bacon, a little grits and some orange juice," Christie said as she swirled the spoon around the grits and brought them to her father's mouth.

No one could have prepared Christie for having to care for her father the way he had cared for her as a child. It broke her heart but she was proud to do it at the same time.

"Umm hmm..." her father replied as he ate a spoonful of grits. "How are you, baby girl?"

Christie shrugged. The last thing she wanted to do was to worry her father about her aunt's strange behavior. Evelyn had been even more hot and cold than normal and Christie was more than confused with her. Still, her father was dealing with bigger issues than a strange aunt-niece relationship.

"I'm better now that I'm here," Christie smiled widely.

The two made small talk while she fed him breakfast and watched a little bit of television. When she stood to clear his tray, her father grabbed her wrist. She glanced down and saw his eyes pleading with her, but no words came from his mouth.

"Daddy, what's wrong? What is it?" Christie asked as she sat down in the chair and leaned forward. Her heart began to race as thoughts danced in her head about what could be wrong.

"Baby girl, I want you to listen to me," he said clearly. "If anything happens to me, I want you to stick by your family."

Christie scrunched her face up in confusion as her father waved his hands.

"I know you and Evelyn haven't always gotten along but, baby girl, she's family."

She heard what he was saying, but she didn't think he knew half of how horrible Evelyn could be. Still, he was her father and she respected him enough to hear him out.

"But," he continued in a lowered his voice, "I want you to be smart."

"What do you mean, Daddy?" Christie asked, sitting up in her chair, intrigued.

"The only person I want you to trust right now is Deborah. That's it."

"But, Daddy, you just said—"

"I know what I said, Christie. I want you to stick with your family but I don't want you to do so blindly. Keep your eyes open and pay attention."

Christie saw it was causing her father pain to tell her not to trust his sisters but, the truth of the matter was, Christie hadn't trusted them for some time. Her father's advice was just confirmation.

"Daddy, I don't understand."

"It could be all this medicine they have me on, but ever since my house was robbed, something hasn't seemed right, baby girl. I don't know what it is. All I can say is the only one I want you to trust right now is Deborah. I think that robbery was a sham and I can't say for sure, but I feel like the people closest to me are the ones who know the most about it."

Christie felt like someone had hit her in her chest. She'd had her difficulties with her Aunt Evelyn, but she would never think that she or her Aunt Angelica would do anything to hurt her father—physically or emotionally. Now, as she sat staring into her father's eyes, she knew she needed to pay closer attention to everything and everyone.

Later in the day the doctor led her into a room with her aunts to discuss her father's condition and treatment options.

"Mrs. Adams, we waited until you arrived to talk to you all about your father's diagnosis. Your aunts thought that was best," the mousy doctor said, staring at Christie.

"Okay, so tell me," Christie replied as she glanced over at her aunts, who were seemingly calm, then back to the doctor.

"We've determined your father has amyloidosis as well as congestive heart failure," the doctor said as if she knew exactly what that meant.

"Amylo…what?" Christie asked quickly.

"Amyloidosis. It's a very rare disease where one or more organ systems in the body build up deposits of abnormal proteins, known as amyloid. The Amyloidosis Foundation is an excellent resource to learn more information about the disease."

Christie's eyes began to fill with tears. It was so confusing and she wasn't sure what to make of it. She looked to her aunts and saw them staring at the doctor.

"I don't even know what that means. What…what's that mean for my father?" Christie asked.

The doctor looked back at his folder and then answered, "Your father has probably had this disease for nearly ten years, Mrs. Adams. Coupled with his congestive heart fail—"

"He's had it for ten years? What do you mean? How is that even possible? My father went to the doctor every year. How could we just be finding out?" Christie interrupted the doctor.

"Mrs. Adams, your father knew about his congestive heart failure and has been seeing a specialist. There's a possibility the specialist overlooked the amyloidosis because his concern and attention was focused on the congestive heart failure. Your father may not have told you because he didn't know how or hadn't fully accepted the diagnosis himself. Amyloidosis is very rare, Mrs. Adams. Amyloidosis and congestive heart together spell trouble. From your father's charts, it looks like the treatment he was receiving from the specialist was minimal because of the stage of his illness. We're going to continue doing what we can but we needed to alert you to his condition so you can think about your next steps."

"What do you mean next steps?" Christie looked at her aunts. Why weren't they upset? The only next step Christie was concerned with was getting her father out of the hospital.

"Mrs. Adams, I understand your aunts talked to you about Tyson Hospice. We need a decision as soon as possible on whether you choose to send your father there or if you'd rather keep him here."

"We're sending him wherever he needs to go to get better."

The doctor lowered his head and took a very long breath, letting Christie know what he was about to say was not easy.

"At this point, Mrs. Adams, it's not about your father getting better; it's more about keeping him comfortable."

"Shouldn't he stay here, where you all can monitor him?" Christie asked through her tears.

The doctor was about to reply when her Aunt Evelyn spoke up.

"Kenneth needs to go to this hospice. It's the best thing for him. If they're saying that he's going to pass away regardless of what is done, we want him to be comfortable," Evelyn said, sounding like an infomercial.

"What do you recommend, doctor?" Christie asked, hoping he had something better to say.

"Well, in my professional opin—" the doctor started before Evelyn interrupted.

"Kenneth is going to Tyson's Hospice and that's that. If he's going to die, he needs to be comfortable."

Her aunt was saying that her father was going to die. Christie felt the tears on her cheeks before she realized she was crying. Her heart was breaking with every second she remained seated. She had to get out of there.

"I've got to go," Christie said as she grabbed her purse and jacket and bolted for the door.

"We're going to tell Kenneth in a few minutes, if you want to be there," Angelica said, not looking in Christie's direction. Christie wanted to be there, but she couldn't. She was barely able to keep it together for herself, let alone anyone else.

Christie high-tailed it down the stark white hallway and headed to her rental car. As she sat in the warming car, her mind played back memories with her father. She wasn't ready to have only memories to feast on; she wanted her father there to laugh, joke and talk with.

When she arrived at Evelyn's house, she immediately retreated to the guest bedroom. It was hard to force her eyes closed but once she did, it felt like she hadn't closed them in years. Not until she felt hands shaking her shoulders, did she pull out of her deep sleep.

"I made dinner. Come eat," Evelyn said sharply as she headed back to the kitchen.

Christie was not in the mood for dinner or conversation with her aunt but she knew she needed to eat. Dragging herself into the kitchen, Christie sat at the table and waited as her aunt plopped a plate of spaghetti in front of her.

"You're welcome," she said before Christie had a chance to thank her.

"Thank you, Aunt Evelyn," Christie said smartly.

The two ate in silence until Evelyn spoke. "I don't think it was a good idea for you to storm out of the hospital like that, Christie. Your father needed you and you left us to console him."

Christie almost choked on her food. Calmly, she set her fork down, took a sip of water and looked at her aunt.

"Aunt Evelyn, I hope both of y'all understand just how hard it was for me to hear that a doctor thinks my father won't make it. So excuse me for not being able to hold it together," Christie said in a smug tone.

"This affects all of us. You need to be considerate."

At this point, Christie was doing more than biting her tongue.

"Be considerate, Aunt Evelyn? What's this really about? I've been up at that hospital fifteen to twenty hours a day and only coming home to nap. But now I'm not considerate?" Christie shouted angrily.

"Listen, I overheard you talking to Anthony about how you were thinking about staying in a hotel. I talked to your father about it and he couldn't believe how you're treating your own family—like we're strangers."

Christie's face was piercing hot. She knew her aunt was capable of anything but she couldn't believe she would go this far to anger her and upset her father.

"You had no right," Christie said.

By now, Christie knew her aunt's ploy was to get a reaction and as much as she didn't want to give her one she knew she had to in order to feel good about herself.

"Aunt Evelyn, I had a private conversation with my husband and you invaded my privacy. Ask yourself why I would want to stay somewhere else. All you've done recently is pick fights and act rude. Why would I want to stay here? What you don't need to do is involve my father in any of this."

Evelyn took her plate to the sink then turned to face Christie.

"Angelica and I have been talking and we think the best thing right now is for Kenneth to go to the hospice center."

Christie stood up, slowly allowing her napkin to hit the floor. "If my father stays in the hospital they can watch over him more closely and he has a better chance of recovering. The hospice is the place to send him if we want him to die," Christie said as she headed back to her room.

Her head was spinning. Did her aunts want her father to die quickly? It couldn't be! Pacing her room, Christie contemplated calling Anthony but knew it would take more out of her to tell the entire story than it would to just journal it.

Christie had recently taken up journaling and had found it to be therapeutic. Reaching into her purse, she fished out a pen and her red journal and quickly began jotting down notes from that day.

"I can't believe my aunts are acting like this isn't their brother lying in that bed. I feel like I'm the only one going to bat for my daddy," Christie wrote as she let her pen linger over the paper.

"Baby girl," her father said as she snapped out of her dream of the previous day's events.

"Sorry, Daddy. What'd you say?" Christie said as she turned and faced her father.

He was aware she now knew about his illness but neither of them was up to talking about the elephant in the room.

"Are you still going to lunch with Deborah?" Kenneth asked with a slight grin. It was one of the first times she had seen her father smile since being in the hospital.

"Yeah, I'll call her to confirm," Christie replied as she sat back in the chair.

"You and Deborah going out for lunch, huh? I think you'll really like her, baby girl. Your aunts, well you know how they can be. They don't really care for her but Deborah's a good woman."

Christie smiled as she dialed Deborah and verified their lunch in a few hours. She didn't really feel like meeting Deborah or talking about her with her father, but she knew that was out of her control.

"Let's talk about you, Daddy. How are you feeling?" Christie said, holding his hand and staring into his eyes.

A couple hours later, after talking to her father about his illness and her hesitancy about going to lunch with Deborah, Christie felt better about getting to know the woman who had stolen her father's heart.

"You picked a great place," Deborah said as she sat in the booth across from Christie.

"I love their bread," Christie said with a smile. She had grown up going to The Chop Shop on "dates" with her father.

"Me too, girl," Deborah said as she moved a piece of hair away from her face.

After giving their drink orders the silence between them became so awkward it was a relief when the waitress finally returned. Christie ordered a cheeseburger with barbeque sauce and Deborah ordered shrimp alfredo before they sipped their drinks and began to talk.

"I don't know what's going through your aunts' minds," Deborah said.

"Excuse me?"

"I'm sorry, I know they're your aunts but I swear sometimes I think they're out to get Kenneth, not to fight for him."

Christie wasn't sure if Deborah was a mind reader but she wasn't agreeing with anything. She was still feeling Deborah out and in no rush to join sides with her without knowing why she didn't trust her aunts.

"Your father asked me to stay close to you if anything happened to him. I don't know about those sisters of his, though. Since that robbery they've been acting really strange."

Christie narrowed her eyes and listened intently, trying to remember every detail to journal later that evening.

"I've been here for your father day in and day out since he became ill and it still doesn't seem to be enough for them."

"My family has an interesting dynamic," Christie said as she took another sip of her water and thought about what to say.

If her aunts didn't trust Deborah and Deborah didn't trust her aunts, who was Christie to trust? She saw Deborah's mouth moving but didn't hear anything she said because her mind was trying to make sense of the puzzle developing before her.

"You can trust me," she heard Deborah say before she stopped listening.

When the puzzle was solved Christie would understand exactly why her father had given her specific instructions to trust and stay close to Deborah.

Until then, she had a cheeseburger to slay and a mystery to solve.

Eighteen

Christie stirred her water and slowly watched as the ice drifted around the frosted glass. She wasn't in the mood to meet with her attorneys but, as she'd learned, she had to do a lot of things she didn't want to do.

Gone were her hours of getting ready in the morning, caring about her appearance. Christie barely felt like applying a coat of lip-gloss these days. Her meticulous wardrobe was now replaced with comfortably fitting skinny jeans and an oversized shirt. Anthony had tried his best to get her to exercise but, like much else in her life, Christie didn't care about it anymore. Her main focus had become the theft of her father's money, what really happened leading up to his death, and how her twisted aunts were involved. Even her health had taken a back seat to those mysteries. After her doctor's visit and blood tests when she fainted, Anthony had to force Christie to make an appointment to get the test results but she'd blown that off three times.

When Christie finally went in and met with Dr. Silver about her test results, she realized that she couldn't cling to life as she had previously known it. While the diagnosis wasn't fatal, Christie was far from relieved with the results.

Still, she tried her best to keep her mind focused off of herself and onto the situation with her father's money.

"Hey," Christie said to her attorneys, Grace Humphries and Bill Spectrum of the top law firm in the area. With Janice's help, Christie had been lucky enough to get them to take on her case. Though things with Bobby were slow in producing results, Christie was hopeful that hiring a private investigator and attorneys would snap her aunts into shape. Unfortunately they were going about their lives as if nothing had ever happened while Christie was living her life in slow motion.

Grace Humphries had a hard face but a soft disposition. Christie guessed that this worked to her favor in the courtroom. She had stringy blonde hair that stopped at her chin and piercing blue eyes that displayed little emotion. Grace was tall, really tall. Christie figured she probably played volleyball or basketball in college based on her physique and height. Bill Spectrum, on the other hand, was short, nerdy and a bit goofy. His messy brown hair always seemed like it was searching for the right place to lie on his head. Bill sported trifocals that seemed too big and suits that seemed like they belonged to his father. Still, when Bill got going in the courtroom he was a beast. Janice once featured Bill on her show for defending a man whose family had cleaned out his entire life savings while he lay in a coma. Bill won the case and praise for his pit-bull actions. After Janice recommended that Christie meet Grace and Bill to see if the case was a fit, they immediately hit it off.

A month later Christie was sitting in Starbucks waiting to hear why they'd urgently called the meeting.

"Hey, Christie, it's good to see you," Grace said as she set her briefcase down on the table and removed her jacket. Bill nodded and smiled before doing the same.

"How have things been?" Bill asked, leaning back in his chair.

Christie admired how confident Bill was. She had once been that way too but life had dealt her a blow that paralyzed her confidence.

"Everything's okay. I've just been trying my best to piece things together. I ran into my aunt a few weeks ago at the doctor's office. It was a very strange interaction." "You don't think she followed you there, do you?" Grace inquired.

"No. I think it was just fate, or life, or both."

"We wanted to meet with you today because we're nearly ready to file papers to sue your aunts for the theft of your father's money. We just have a few loose ends to tie up and then we're ready to take this to the next level."

It was news Christie had both looked forward to and despised hearing. Everything was happening quickly now. How did they *know* her aunts were responsible? What made them so confident?

"How…I mean…did something happen? The last time we met we just had conspiracy theories. Now we're ready to serve papers?"

Bill grinned as if Christie had asked him the golden question.

"We've discovered your aunts had some kind of relationship with the Tyson Hospice Center. There was some sort of payoff happening between the two. Do you remember when you told us your aunts were pushing for your father being admitted to Tyson Hospice? It appears there was some financial gain on both sides by having your father stay there."

Christie gasped. She knew something had been up but she never would have guessed it would be this.

"With that information and statements from the bank manager, the doctors and you, I think we have a case strong enough to proceed," Grace said.

Christie hung her head. A part of her had wanted them to find nothing wrong; the other half of her knew they would.

"Last night while we were going through some of your father's financials and bank records, we were able to identify some of the purchases made during the time he was hospitalized," Bill explained as he reached in his briefcase and pulled out a single piece of paper. Christie focused on the lines highlighted in yellow.

"You'll see here that a week after your father went into the hospital, a transfer of $95,000 was made to that mysterious New York account. Your father couldn't have made this transfer and, as far as we're concerned, he didn't authorize it either."

Christie ran her hand over the document and rested it on the line showing the transfer. Her heart was leaping into her throat.

"Then if you'll look two lines down we have records of cruises, clothing, electronics and food that were paid for using your father's account. A few more lines further you'll see where more money was transferred to the New York account."

Christie felt like she wanted to cry, but she couldn't. She wasn't sure if it was because she was all cried out or if she was simply too angry to form a tear.

"The kicker, though, was there was a transfer made directly from your father's account to the Tyson Hospice Center. Your father was never a patient so there was no reason such a large payment should have been made to them."

"Your aunts were the only ones with control over his account, correct?" Grace asked.

Christie nodded. She wanted to make sense of it all, but now that it was in front of her, she wasn't so sure that she could handle the truth.

"I know this is a lot to take in but we need to be sure you know everything we've learned. I think you have a very strong probability of winning this case and unless your aunts can explain what happened, it should be a slam dunk," Bill explained.

"I just can't believe it, you know?" Christie said as she lifted her head and stared at her attorneys with confusion in her eyes.

"We have a few more things to verify before we serve the papers and get things rolling. We need to pin down exact details on this mystery account. And Grace told me something that I want clarify with you," Bill whispered as he leaned forward.

"What's that?"

"When you first met with Grace she said you told her about a conversation you had with one of your aunts where they claimed they would "take care of you" if something happened to your father. Do you remember that?"

Christie nodded. Of course, she remembered the conversation. Besides the conversation about transferring Kenneth to the hospice; it had stood out the most to her. Something hadn't seemed right about her aunt promising to "take care of her" if and when her father passed.

"That is both troubling and exciting at the same time," Bill said as he glanced over at Grace who nodded in agreement with her.

"Come again?"

Why on earth would her aunt's strange choice of words be exciting to her attorneys?

"Christie, you have to trust us on this. That exchange is going to help us win this case. I just need you to try to remember any other conversations you had that seemed strange or suspicious and email them over to us ASAP."

Christie knew when to argue and when to do as she was told. "Okay."

"We've got to go, Grace. This is major. Let's go!" Bill exclaimed as he jumped up and headed for the door.

Grace turned and smiled at Christie. "Trust us. We'll be in touch," she said as she grabbed her things and darted after Bill.

The last thing that Christie could do was trust.

"Table for one?"

"Two, please, the other party is parking right now," Christie replied as she smoothed her pants and shirt. She was sure she should have other things on her mind than her conversation with her attorneys, but it was all she could think about.

"You would pick Applebee's of all places," Janice chuckled as she slid into the booth.

Christie looked at her friend and grinned. She looked good, as usual. It made Christie aware of how she looked herself and she started smoothing her hair.

"Can we have two waters to start and I'll have a glass of your house red wine," Janice said to the waiter as he appeared then quickly disappeared.

"Do you want a drink too?" Janice said with a sly grin. She already knew Christie wouldn't be drinking, based on how she looked.

"Goodness, no," Christie replied, waving her friend off.

"It's good to see you…finally," Janice joked as she looked at her menu and before glancing up at Christie.

Christie rolled her eyes. It had been well over a month since she'd seen or talked to Janice because she had been so consumed with everything else in her life.

"Oh hush," Christie laughed as she scanned the menu. She felt hungrier than she had in weeks and everything on the menu sounded delicious.

When the waiter returned, they placed their orders and began chatting about what was going on in their lives.

"So what's been new with you?" Christie asked, beating her friend to the punch.

Janice laughed as she sipped her red wine. "Same ole, same ole. The station's running me ragged with these stories but I guess it's what I signed up for. Oh, and I was approached recently to interview with a station in New York but I don't know…"

Through all the years Christie had known Janice, she had never really seen her troubled about anything. Christie widened her eyes.

"Wow. What do you think? New York is any anchor's dream market, right?"

Janice nodded but didn't answer. Christie guessed it was because Janice would have to vocalize that she was thinking about leaving the city, an area she had grown to love and where she had made a name for herself.

"It's such a great opportunity and women my age who get them are supposed to jump on them quickly," Janice said, finally looking into Christie's eyes, "but Indianapolis is really everything I've known. I know I could handle New York but do I want to?"

"You have to do what's best for you. Don't worry about what you're leaving, Janice. Do you remember when I was getting ready to leave the station and having a panic attack, wondering if I was doing the right thing?" Christie asked.

Janice nodded as she ran her finger along the rim of her wine glass.

"It's exactly the same thing. You can take it or leave it but whatever you choose *you* have to be happy with your decision."

Christie didn't know where her words of wisdom were coming from, but she was happy to help. Janice was, after all, the one Christie had been able to go to when her relationship with Anthony was in shambles from choosing work over love and again when her father passed away. It was the least Christie could do.

Janice smiled with her head down and Christie found herself grinning too. Janice's hair hung effortlessly over her right eye and Christie thought again how put-together Janice looked, even in duress.

"What about you? What's going on in your world?"

Christie shrugged. She was still trying to decipher everything that happened just a few hours earlier with her attorneys and wasn't sure if she was ready to spill it all to Janice. She hadn't even told Anthony.

"Let's see...I met with the lawyers today and they're close to serving papers to get this lawsuit underway so I guess I'm nervous and on edge about that. I have been sleeping way too much lately. And let's not even get into how my face is breaking out," Christie blurted out with a laugh.

Janice set her glass down and leaned forward.

"Before you go to court we're going to *have* to do something about... well...you know..." Janice said with a disgusted yet hilarious look on her face.

"About what?" Christie said as she cocked her head to the side looking at Janice and then back at herself. She didn't need her friend to tell her what she already knew. She had gained weight and looked a mess.

"This whole hobo-chic, rolled-out-of-bed look you have going on. This isn't *you*," Janice giggled.

It was true. Christie was much more of a girly girl when it came down to it. She liked her massages, manicures, pedicures and getting her hair done twice a month. Usually, her hair would hang bone straight to her shoulders with curls just framing her face and she wore enough makeup to make people notice her beauty. Today, though, she had pulled her hair back in a loose ponytail and her only makeup was a coat of lip gloss. Christie was beautiful, but it was apparent she was dealing with more than how she looked.

"I know...," Christie said as the waiter appeared with their food.

"What's Anthony saying about all of this? The weight gain, the clothes—all of it?"

"He wants me to be happy and he knows this isn't bringing me any happiness. We've started walking in the evenings and I like that. I just can't bring myself to work out for hours at the gym right now. My mind isn't there."

The two ate and made small talk throughout the meal. When they were finished, Janice drank the last of her wine and looked over at her friend.

"Once this is all over, we're going to look back on it and laugh. I promise," she said as her phone began buzzing.

"This better not be the office," Janice growled. As soon as her eyes saw the caller ID, they grew big as saucers and she held up one finger signaling Christie not to talk.

Christie sipped her water and watched what seemed to be a frantic call. When Janice hung up, Christie was intrigued.

Janice stood up and pulled Christie with her toward the door.

"Who was that?" Christie asked as she slapped down cash for both meals.

"Come on! Come on!" Janice said, tugging her friend. When they reached the parking lot, Christie pulled free and yelled, "Janice Goldberg, what in the world has gotten into you?"

"That was Bobby. He said he'd been trying to call you all morning but your phone was going straight to voicemail."

"I turned it off when I met with my lawyers and just forgot to turn it back on."

"Listen, he found information about the New York bank account. He knows whose name is on it."

"Whose name?"

"He said the account is in the name of Michael Whitfield, Jr."

"The account is in Junior's name?"

Christie's hands shook as she called Grace and relayed the news Bobby had uncovered.

After her call, she vomited.

Nineteen

"I just need to get away," Christie heard herself say as she stuffed the last of her things into her duffle bag.

Anthony understood everything she was going through and she knew he wouldn't fight her on leaving for a few days.

"Anything you need to do, babe," he said as he sat on the bed watching her pack.

Christie felt the need to leave to clear her head. Between the attorneys, private investigators and her health, she felt she was on the brink of losing it. She needed the comfort of the one place she felt at home—her father's house.

"I'll be back on Sunday. I love you," Christie said as she leaned forward to plant a deep, long kiss on Anthony's lips. She did love her husband, probably more than ever. Anthony "got her" and enabled her to focus on everything in front of her.

"You sure you don't want me to go with you? I can always reschedule my meetings and get away from the office for a few days."

Christie smiled widely, feeling her face get warm. Anthony still did it for her.

"No, babe. You have that important meeting and you've been preparing for six months. I'll be fine. I just need some alone time at my dad's house."

Anthony shook his head and went down the stairs to load Christie's things into the car for the familiar trek to the airport.

"Are you going to get a hotel room or are you going to stay at your father's? Is the electricity even on?" Anthony asked as he pulled out into traffic.

She had completely forgotten the electricity was turned off shortly after his funeral.

"I forgot. So I guess I'll get a hotel when I get there. It's not like I can call up Evelyn or Angelica and ask for a place to crash, right?" Christie laughed awkwardly as she looked out of the window.

"Yeah, I wouldn't recommend doing that. I might never see you again," Anthony chuckled.

Christie smirked, but a bit of what Anthony said hurt. It was true, but that didn't take away the pain that accompanied her current reality.

Sensing Christie's change in attitude, Anthony quickly changed the subject.

"So what are you planning to do when you get there?" he said as he eyed the signs for the airport approach.

"I don't really have too much planned. I just feel the need to be as close as possible to my father right now and his house seems like the best place to do that."

"Did you tell Junior you were coming? I'm sure he would love to see you."

Christie had been hesitant to talk to Junior after learning his name was on the mysterious bank account in New York. Still, following her heart, she pulled out her cell phone and sent him a text saying she'd be in Chicago for the weekend.

While Christie and Junior didn't speak every day, they could feel when the other was off; Christie was sure Junior felt the distance.

"I sent him a text and told him, but I don't even know if I want to see him," Christie sighed as they turned towards the departure terminal.

Anthony just nodded. He wanted to say the right thing but he knew anything he said would just further complicate everything Christie *thought* made sense. If he told her to give Junior a chance to explain, it would seem like he thought it wasn't plausible for him to have been involved; if he told her to stay away from him, it seemed like he was saying Junior was guilty.

"Whatever you choose to do, babe. Just remember this entire situation has taught us everything that looks one way isn't always that way."

The two got out of the car, hugged and kissed before Christie disappeared into the airport with her duffle and laptop bag on her shoulders. While Christie went through the TSA search, her eyes caught the attention of a young girl that looked to be no older than six years old with caramel skin and dark freckles adorning her face. Next to her stood a tall, dapper man Christie assumed to be her father.

"Daddy, come on! I want to get a pretzel!" the little girl giggled as she skipped to the end of the line and patiently waited for her shoes and other belongings to come out of the TSA conveyer belt.

"Hold on, princess. We have to get our things," her father said with a proud gleam in his eye.

The little girl's hair was in a curly afro adorned with a beautiful bow hanging to the side of her head. She looked vivacious and was definitely a handful for her father.

"'Okay, Daddy," the little girl said with excitement.

Christie couldn't take her eyes off the duo because they reminded her so much of her and Kenneth when she was younger. The two of them would set out on trips together and it seemed like the rest of the universe didn't matter.

The father must have noticed Christie staring because he cleared his throat and grinned.

"Do you have children?" he asked.

Christie shook her head, "Oh no, not yet. Your daughter's beautiful."

The gentleman smiled so widely he exposed all thirty-two of his teeth. He was definitely a proud father.

"Thank you. We try to do these father-daughter trips to Florida once a year. So my wife can have a break and we can have time for just the two of us."

"That's beautiful. She'll definitely remember these times."

Christie knew what she was talking about; she remembered every trip, every conversation and every gut-busting prank her father had ever showed her on their travels. Like the time they'd traveled from Chicago to New York to catch a play and her father had somehow tricked the waiter into thinking it was Christie's birthday. As a thirteen year old girl, Christie was overly embarrassed but looking back she was so grateful for the memories.

"Oh, there are our things. It was good talking to you. Have a safe trip." The man said as he darted off to grab his daughter.

Christie smiled to herself as she gathered her own things and headed to her gate.

She had a few minutes to spare so she stopped in a store to pick up a bottle of water and a magazine. Just as she paid, she felt her phone buzz and pulled it from her purse to read the text from Junior.

Love to see you. Something's different. We need to talk.

Christie wasn't sure how to reply so she didn't. What would she say? Did you steal money from my dying father with your mom and her sister? It was too difficult to fathom, so Christie decided to put off thinking about it.

The flight to Chicago was uneventful. With everything on her mind she barely flipped through her magazine. As they prepared to land she suddenly became nervous. Was it because of who she might run into or because she was going to face her father's house alone? Only time would tell.

After retrieving her bags and her rental car, Christie headed to grab a bite to eat before going to her father's. She still needed to get a hotel room but was anxious to check on the house.

Just as she expected, everything was intact and in order. When she opened the door, everything looked exactly as it had when she had left it a month and a half earlier. She could even smell her father's cologne.

Christie walked around the living room and opened all the blinds so light could shine in. Plopping down on the couch, Christie eyed the fast food she'd picked up and suddenly couldn't bring herself to eat.

"My nerves are bad," Christie laughed nervously as she walked around the house as if she was at a museum.

Stopping at a painting of her father that hung on the wall, Christie felt overwhelmed with emotion. Not a sad sense of emotion where she might bawl her eyes out; she just felt disappointed.

"When are you going to have some grandbabies?" Christie heard her father ask, *replaying a conversation they'd had on numerous occasions.*

"I told you, Anthony and I aren't ready for all that right now," Christie shot back, *offended that her father continued to ask about children when she had other things on her mind.*

"I hope you have some babies while your mother and I can still play with them," Kenneth *joked as she rolled her eyes.*

Snapping out of her daydream, Christie bowed her head and let a few tears fall. All that time she had been fighting having children—something her father desperately wanted—she could have been honoring his wishes. She felt disappointed in herself for being so selfish.

Christie placed one hand on the wall and leaned forward as she cried silently. She knew the feeling of being sad and missing her father, but the feeling of disappointment in missing the opportunity to give her father a grandchild had hit her like a ton of bricks.

"Why couldn't I just have done what he asked?" Christie asked herself as she slid down the wall. Her legs sprawled out and kicked a box in front of her.

With tears clouding her vision, Christie wiped her face and leaned forward to inspect the box. After she and Anthony had packed up most of her father's possessions, there had been a lot of boxes left lying around the house. This had to be one that needed to make its way to the basement or storage.

Flipping it open, Christie gasped as a picture of her dressed in a cap and gown at her kindergarten graduation stared back at her.

"Oh my goodness," she squealed as she picked it up.

In the picture Christie smiled with a snaggletooth grin and her hair in puffy twists peeking out from under the cap. "I remember this day," Christie said to herself. "Daddy took mom and I out to the Chinese buffet and I thought it was the fanciest place on earth."

Running her fingers over her face, Christie wanted to tell her young self to be prepared for everything life might toss her way. She wiped her tears as they continued to slowly fall. The young Christie had no idea how cruel the world would be.

Looking deeper into the box, Christie found plaques, awards and letters of achievement she had received and Kenneth had obviously collected. Her heart dropped. This entire box, filled to the brim, was a sign from her father to let her know that regardless of any disappointment or regrets he thought the world of her.

She pulled out all the papers and pictures and scattered them all over the floor.

My baby girl at Disney World, the back of one picture read.

Me and my Baby Girl, read another.

Christie clutched them all and pulled herself up from the floor. She knew she couldn't mourn anymore over what *had* or *had not* been done; she simply had to focus on what she could now do.

Picking up her cell phone, Christie sent a text to Junior. *Let's meet at the park by my father's house in an hour. We need to talk.*

A quick reply came through. *Okay. See you then.*

Christie knew what she had to do.

She fidgeted nervously on a wooden park bench and waited for Junior to arrive. He was fifteen minutes late and Christie was starting to get impatient. Although it was a beautiful day, Christie hated waiting.

Where are you? Christie text.

I'm sorry Cousin. Michael had me run an errand. I'm on the way.

Christie decided to calm herself down by taking in the beautiful scenery. She looked over at the swing set where she'd played as a child and grinned.

"Hey, babe," Christie said as she picked up her ringing cell phone.

"Hey to you, too," Anthony replied. Christie could tell he was smiling. "You doing good? Have you been by your father's house yet?"

"Yeah, I went by there about an hour ago. I found some boxes babe, which showed me how proud my father was of me. I mean, I knew he was proud of me but to see it just sitting there, like it was waiting for me, had me in tears."

"That's good, Chris. You know your father thought the world of you. On our wedding day he told me that if I couldn't measure up to half the person you were, that I should just leave."

Christie laughed at her father's antics. He had always been one to speak his mind and cover it with a bit of humor.

"I text Junior and told him I was here. We're supposed to be meeting in the park but he's running late and—" Christie said as she stopped mid-sentence when she saw the person walking towards her.

"What's wrong, Christie?" Anthony inquired, sensing a change in his wife's tone.

"I'll call you back," Christie replied, not giving him a chance to reply before she hung up.

Standing in front of her was Angelica's husband, Michael.

"What are you doing here?" Christie asked, standing up.

"We need to talk. Junior told me you were here," Michael said as he motioned for Christie to sit back on the bench with him.

"I'll stand, thank you."

"Fine, have it your way." Michael shrugged as he crossed his legs. "All of this needs to stop and it needs to stop now. This is one big misunderstanding and you, of all people Christie, need to understand that and call off all these over-the-top antics you've thrown at us. We're family," Michael finished as he finally looked up at an astonished Christie.

She couldn't believe the words coming out of his mouth.

"You have some nerve, you know that? You all do."

"*We* have some nerve, Christie? You have attorneys and are talking about lawsuits over something you have no clue about. It's all rather sad. Your father would be disappointed in you."

That was all she needed to hear to lose her composure. She had neither liked nor disliked Michael but she had shown him the respect he was due because he was married to her aunt. Now, though, that respect was gone.

"Somewhere on your drive over here, you must've bumped your head. My father would be ashamed of *me*? Or do you think he'd be ashamed of the fact that the people closest to him were the very ones who stole from him when he was dying?" Christie shouted loudly.

Michael cleared his throat to respond.

"Shut up. You listen to me. If you thought you were going to come down here and bully me into dropping my case, you were wrong. You can go and tell Angelica, Evelyn and whoever else that if this is what family means, I don't want it!" Christie said angrily as she turned to walk away.

"Christie, listen to me," Michael said, approaching Christie. "I'm prepared to write you a check today for $500,000 to make all of this go away."

Christie couldn't believe what she was hearing. Was this fool offering her money stolen from her father? Was he trying to pay her off so they could all pretend nothing had ever happened?

Christie turned and faced Michael, staring into his eyes. Seconds went by before she could formulate a thought.

"You know what? I don't know what's more ironic, the fact that you think I'd take your dirty money after knowing what you all did to my father, or the fact that this seems to be what you're good at."

Michael jumped back and eyed Christie suspiciously.

"You remember Cleveland back in '97, don't you, Michael? What do you think the police there would do if they found out you locked up an innocent man simply to keep him away from your wife?"

Christie could see Michael's face go pale. She had him.

Thankfully, Christie had paid close attention to her father's conversations when she was a child and while they didn't make sense to her then, they were golden now.

"Wh-what…what on earth are you talking about?"

"Oh, you remember Julius Borgen, don't you? You arrested him in the summer of 1997 because Aunt Angelica was about to leave you for him. Or did you think I was clueless about that? I didn't know at the time that he was Junior's real father but now it all makes sense. How do you think Aunt Angelica, Junior and your police family will feel when they find out you planted drugs on Julius and had him put away? You knew he was a felon too, didn't you? You knew he'd go away for a long time."

Michael's face had gone from Casper the friendly ghost to devil red.

"You have no idea what you're talking about, little girl."

"And neither do you, Michael. So next time you want to try to buy your wrongs to make them right, make sure your closet is clean."

Christie gave Michael one last look before she walked away, leaving him fuming.

On her way to her car, she saw Junior pull into the parking lot.

"Where you going? Sorry I was running late!" he shouted as he jumped out of his car and headed towards Christie who was walking faster than speeding bullet.

"Leave me alone, Junior."

Junior stopped mid-jog and looked at his cousin. Something was definitely wrong.

"What happened? What's going on?" he asked, looking around.

Christie ignored him, unlocked her car and slid in before putting the car in reverse and backing out.

"Chris! What's happening? You asked me to meet you here. I was running behind and you're pissed? At least tell me what I did."

Christie rolled down her window and stared at her cousin. She loved him but if he had anything to do with any of this she was very much over him like the rest of her family.

"Are you in it with them?"

Confusion covered Junior's face.

"In what with who?"

"Was this a set-up? Why did Michael show up today instead of you?"

Junior continued looking baffled. "Michael was here? I didn't know he was coming. He asked me where I was going. I told him I was going to meet you and he asked me to make a stop for him. That's it. I don't know anything else."

Christie believed him, but she was beyond mad. She couldn't talk rationally about anything right now, especially not with family.

"You need to find out how you're linked to all of this, Junior. They've gotten you in way over your head and you don't even know you got tossed in the water."

With that, Christie sped off. Her heart hurt but her mind hurt more from thinking about how much her heart hurt. There had to be some truth in the saying that love is blind and makes the best of us fools. As least that's how Christie rationalized her uncharacteristic trust of the Whitfield clan.

Twenty

Christie was fat. Not thick and curvy cute, just fat. It had been months since she'd worked out and it showed. Her stomach was bloated, her face was pudgy, her breasts were larger than they'd ever been before and her skin was riddled with breakouts.

Christie knew Anthony wanted to say something but hadn't out of respect for her and everything she was going through.

"Babe, you know we can still go for our walks in the evening, if you'd like," Anthony said as he sat on the bed watching ESPN, while Christie looked at herself in the full-length mirror.

She turned from one side to the other and grimaced. She liked being able to eat whatever she wanted whenever she wanted, but she hated looking at herself in the mirror. Following her father's death, she'd given herself time to grieve and swore she'd get her body back in order shortly after. She was creeping up on the deadline and wasn't feeling any more compelled to bust a sweat.

"Yeah, we probably should," Christie replied over her shoulder as she walked into her closet and searched for something to wear.

"Are you and Janice going for drinks today?" Anthony questioned.

"Mmm hmm…you know the drill," Christie kidded as she chose a pair of tights and an oversized blouse that she knew wouldn't make her look as heavy as she felt.

"Remember we're going to go out for dinner tonight with one of my clients and his wife, so don't get wasted or anything," Anthony jokingly said with a chuckle.

Christie giggled at the thought and threw on her clothes before walking over to Anthony and taking his hand.

"Do you like me fat?" Christie heard herself ask. She didn't know why she'd asked the question, but she was curious to know the answer.

Since they'd met, Anthony had only known Christie to be fit and beautiful. Now he was being introduced to the sloppy, overweight Christie and she wondered if he was still attracted to her.

"Babe, you're sexy to me whether you're 100 pounds or 200 pounds," Anthony said, holding her hand tightly. "You know that, right?"

She was worrying for nothing. Anthony had seen her at her best and at her worst but still loved her like she was a million dollars.

"I love you," Christie cooed as she leaned forward and kissed Anthony on his forehead.

"I love you too," Anthony replied as he placed his hands on Christie's body and caressed her softly. "Now, hurry up so you can come back to me."

Christie giggled like a schoolgirl before grabbing her purse and heading out the door.

By the time she arrived at the restaurant, Janice already had two empty margarita glasses in front of her with a basket of chips and salsa.

"Well, I see you got started without me," Christie grinned as she slid into the booth across from her friend.

Janice's face said everything that no one else would say aloud to Christie—she was huge.

"Christie," Janice said with wide eyes, "you've gotten so…"

"Big?" Christie asked as she flagged down a waitress to order a virgin margarita and a glass of water with lime.

"I thought you said you and Anthony were walking and—"

"I have too much going on right now to focus on walking and exercising for hours at a time. You know my family has practically disowned me, right?"

She knew Christie's family situation but never expected to hear she'd been disowned.

"Not your mother, too, right?" Janice whispered as she leaned forward.

"Oh, Lord no. My mom has been my rock through all of this. It's the Whitfield side of my family that has declared they will have nothing to do with me."

When it had initially happened, Christie had been hurt and shocked that *they* were the ones disowning *her*. Now, though, she was just nonchalant with it. The day the letter arrived Christie had been flat ironing her hair in preparation for a romantic dinner with Anthony. The Fed Ex deliveryman rang the doorbell and asked Christie to sign for an envelope.

"Dear Christie,

You are our brother's daughter but we will no longer have anything to do with you. Your actions have embarrassed us and disgraced everything our family has strived for. We are disappointed in everything you have done over these past few months and think it's best if we no longer communicate. We will always have the connection of blood but anything beyond that will be severed.

Signed,

The Whitfield Family"

Nothing could surprise Christie anymore she thought as she tossed the letter on the kitchen counter. This had to be some sort of reverse psychology they were pulling on her and she wasn't falling for it.

Christie tried not to think about that day too much but as Janice sat in front of her wondering how her friend could have let herself go *that* much Christie shared what she had been going through.

"Christie I'm so sorry. I can't believe this is happening to you of all people. Did you get things situated with Junior? Did you talk to him?" Janice asked as she sipped her margarita.

Christie had spoken to Junior but it was before the letter arrived and she wasn't sure where he stood on that matter. When they'd talked, Christie didn't tell Junior his name was on the mystery account in New York. She wanted his mother to tell him. She owed him that at least.

Christie did however tell him about the stolen money, the attorneys and the lies.

"Chris, you realize what you're accusing them of, right? You know they wouldn't do anything like that. It has to be some sort of big mistake," Junior had said as they sat in her father's home after their run-in at the park.

"You sound like them, Junior. I'm not crazy and you knew my father. You knew how much of a stickler he was when it came to his finances. Do you really think he had only $1,100 in his bank account and that's it? Nothing's adding up but you know what? It will," Christie said, feeling herself getting angry.

She knew where Junior's loyalty lay but it was hard to have one of her closest relatives tell her she was wrong about something when she knew she was so right.

"You don't have to be on my side and you don't have to believe me. I don't care. I'm doing this for the principle of the matter. This isn't right and the truth will be exposed."

Junior rubbed his chin for a few seconds before cutting to the chase, "What did you mean when you said they had me in over my head?"

"You need to ask them, Junior. As a matter of fact you need to ask your mom, Aunt Evelyn *and* Michael what they're hiding from you."

Christie was fed up with hiding everyone's secrets and then being accused of being a liar and troublemaker.

"Chris, if you know something you need to tell me."

Christie shook her head, stood up and walked to the front door. "I need to be alone and you need to figure things out. If you need someone to talk to, I'm here. If they decide to be honest with you, and it coincides with what I'm telling you, I'm here," Christie said as she opened the door and watched her cousin slowly walk out.

It hurt her heart but she was done trying to prove the truth to people who only wanted to live with a lie. Shortly after Junior left, she called the airline and booked a flight home for the next day. She had bitten off way more than she could chew.

Christie replayed the conversation with Junior to Janice who could only shake her head in disbelief.

"When you were at your father's did you get any closure? I know it was hard for you."

"It was hard at first but, you know, seeing how much my father loved me made it much easier. The last visit to his house, one of his neighbors came by and told me that he was sorry about my loss and he wanted to extend his help."

"Help with what?"

"Well, he saw people moving things from the house during the time the alleged burglary was happening. He said he heard about the burglary afterwards but didn't connect what he'd seen with it. After I told him everything that was going on, he said he'd be more than happy to testify."

Janice hooted so loudly Christie cowered in embarrassment, "That's great. I'll bet that guy's testimony will put another nail in that coffin."

Christie tried to mask her smile.

"Excuse me, miss. Is your name Christie Whitfield-Adams?" the waitress tried her best to whisper in the noisy restaurant.

"Who wants to know?" Janice asked.

"There's a man outside who is asking for you. We tried to tell him to come in but he says it's important that he sees you privately."

Christie's heart started racing. Was it Anthony? Was it Bobby? Was it Michael?

"Do you want me to go with you? This could be trouble," Janice said with a raised eyebrow.

Christie shook her head and walked to the front of the restaurant. She had come this far on faith so she wasn't about to be scared off by whatever her mystery guest had for her.

As she stepped out of the restaurant, cool air met her and her hair whipped across her face. She didn't see anyone, but as she turned to walk back into the restaurant, she spotted him.

"I need to talk. I know the truth…at least about Michael not being my father. I think I've pieced the situation with Uncle Kenneth together." Junior said as his watering eyes traveled from the ground to his cousin's face.

Hundreds of miles away from home, Junior had finally been told the truth. Christie wondered how much of it, though.

By the time Christie and Junior arrived back at her house it was dark. Christie gave Junior the opportunity to tell her what he'd learned. The two sat close on the couch as she prepared herself for what she was going to hear. Eventually, Junior slid to the floor and patted the spot next to him as if to tell his cousin to join him.

"I guess a part of me always knew Michael wasn't my father. That wasn't as shocking as finding out about the bank account. It's all a little too much to digest right now."

Christie shared everything she knew and hoped her cousin would see that, despite what people were saying, she wasn't losing her mind.

"I wouldn't say they stole money from my father if I had a shadow of a doubt that they hadn't. They're my *aunts*, my blood." Christie said as she dropped her head. "That's why I wanted you to get their version of the truth from them…if they were going to tell you. How'd you even get them to talk?"

Junior shrugged. "I told my mom I was taking all my things and they'd never seen me again unless I heard some form of the truth…about everything. At first she tried to act like this had been some elaborate scheme to make her and Aunt Evelyn look bad, but after I broke down everything I'd heard, everything I'd witnessed and everything I'd felt, she started singing like a bird."

Christie took a deep breath.

"So the fact of the matter is that in their eyes, they did nothing wrong. They cared for Uncle Kenneth and they did what *he* would've wanted them to do with his money. Of course, they didn't have an explanation as to why they did it so secretively, but that's how they're thinking."

"And what about the lie they told about Michael being your father?"

Junior blew air out as he put his hands on top of his head. "I don't think I'll ever know the full truth and I'm okay with that. It's almost like I can't miss what I've never had."

Christie admired Junior's positive thinking and she wished she could have a dose of it. She wished she didn't care about what those closest to her had done to her and to her father's legacy, but she did care, a whole lot.

Sensing his cousin's mood shift, Junior looked up at her and cleared his throat.

"You know that no matter what, you're my cousin, right? They might be done with you, but I'm not," Junior said, slowly piecing his words together.

Junior was hurt and Christie could tell it in his slow speech and movement. He was trying to put away everything he thought was real and adjust to knowing it was not.

They bonded over the situation, finally falling asleep on the living room floor after talking for hours. Anthony had always liked Junior so he didn't bat an eye when Christie asked if he could stay with them for a few weeks while he cleared his head. He eventually returned to Angelica's, promising he would move closer to Christie in time.

Junior and Christie had both been betrayed and Christie wondered if either of their knowledge of the betrayals would spark a change in Evelyn and Angelica.

Christie knew the answer, but she hoped she was wrong.

Twenty One

Christie adjusted the hips of her tight skirt and grimaced. She wanted to blurt out that she felt disgusting but she knew that would change nothing.

"Where are you headed today?" Anthony asked as he walked past his wife and headed towards the bed.

Christie looked over her shoulder at her husband and smiled.

"I'm going to stop by the office for a few hours," Christie said as she winked. "I wish I could be so lucky to lie in bed all day like you."

"I haven't taken a day off in months, babe. The only thing I'm about to do is watch my eyelids as I sleep."

Christie laughed and shook her head. Even when she felt horrible, she could count on him to make her feel like she was on top of her game.

"How long are you going to stay today? They can't possibly need you to do much. You haven't been in the office in months."

Christie knew Anthony had become used to her being at home resting and getting her mind clear, but she needed to start back to work even if only for a few hours a day. The fact of the matter was that she hadn't been to work since her father's death. Her bosses understood what she was going through but she felt a need to show them she was still alive and kicking. She needed a sense of normalcy back in her life and working part-time would give her just that. Luckily for Christie she had a supportive and resourceful team that had covered her public relations duties easily. She hadn't planned to be gone this long so she appreciated their support.

"I told you I'm going to start part-time so I'll probably be there until noon. Is that okay with my big baby?" Christie cooed as she playfully blew her husband kisses.

Anthony grinned. She knew he was putty when she blew him kisses.

Christie walked into the bathroom and looked at her bloated face. The stress of the lawsuit was physically turning her into someone she couldn't recognize. Still, she smiled and pressed on. As she examined her almond-shaped eyes and the bags under them, the house phone rang loudly in the bedroom.

"Babe, get that," Christie said as she slathered moisturizer on her face.

"Are you serious?" Christie heard Anthony holler.

She darted from the bathroom and narrowed her eyes to see what was going on. Her heart raced as she stared at her husband's face for a sign of what was happening. Anthony's handsome face was a mix of shock and excitement causing Christie to yelp.

"What's happening? What's wrong, babe?" Anthony held the phone from his face and covered the mouth of it before whispering to his wife. "It's your attorneys. The police have arrested Evelyn and Angelica."

Christie closed the laptop on her desk and took a deep breath. She definitely wanted to stay home after the call from her attorneys that morning, but decided she was already dressed so she might as well make her way to work.

"Are you about to call it a day?" Christie's boss asked as he passed her desk.

Christie had really lucked out having Sebastian as a boss. He was the Vice President of Media Relations and kept everything running smoothly in Christie's department. According to Sebastian, his elderly grandfather had been taken advantage of by family members and died with less than fifty cents in the bank. Because of this, Sebastian more than understood when Christie needed to work from home or on some days not work at all.

"Yeah, I think so."

"Keep us updated," Sebastian said as he tapped her desk and walked away.

Sebastian didn't ask too many questions and he didn't give long drawn-out responses. Christie liked that, especially when half the time she didn't feel like talking about the thoughts racing through her mind.

Christie got into her car and sat in silence for a few minutes. Her mind had been playing with her all day. On one hand she was satisfied and excited that her aunts had been arrested, but on the other hand she felt bad. Christie knew her father would not have been happy about his sisters' arrests but she also knew he would have been livid to know everything that had led to it.

Replaying the conversation with her lawyers had Christie on edge. She closed her eyes and envisioned the scene they had described to her from the officers' accounts of the arrest.

Evelyn had been standing in her bedroom, searching for something to wear from the plethora of recently acquired clothes when the officers banged on the door. She answered the door in her tee shirt and jogging pants and the police got right to business.

"Evelyn Robinson?" the officer asked. He could have been a professional model, with his chiseled features, low haircut and beautiful chocolate-colored skin.

"Yes?" Evelyn replied with curiosity. How did they know her name and why were they at her door? She thought this had something to do with the multiple break-ins that had been occurring in her neighborhood.

"I'm Officer Hamilton and this is my partner, Officer Delany," he said as he nodded towards his scrawny partner. "You're under arrest for theft. Please place your hands behind your back."

"I'm under arrest for theft? You have the wrong person. I've never stolen anything in my life. You're going to be in big trouble once I find out who your supervisor is," Evelyn threatened as she prepared to slam the door.

Hamilton put his foot in her door to stop her from closing it and stated, "Ma'am, either you're going to come with us easily or we're going to make a scene."

Evelyn jerked her head back and rolled her eyes. "I will *not* go easily so if you want to arrest me on some fake charges, you'd better have an army with you," Evelyn yelled as she turned and walked away. She was starting to get spooked. Something felt wrong.

The officers followed her into the kitchen where Evelyn picked up the phone and dialed Angelica's number.

"No answer. Where are you Angelica?" Evelyn angrily shouted before turning to face the officers. "I'm not going."

"Ms. Robinson, you already have charges of theft against you. If you refuse to come with us, we will also charge you with resisting arrest and it will be a much bigger deal than it needs to be," Officer Delany said in a deep voice. He looked like he could be related to Andy Griffith except he was much skinnier.

Evelyn dropped her head and wondered how she was going to explain this to her neighbors, friends and family.

Officer Hamilton was growing impatient. "Let's go," he said, reaching for her wrist and placing it behind her back. Her other wrist soon followed and before she knew it, she was in the back of one of the patrol cars.

"Where are we going? Don't we have to go downtown?" Evelyn shouted as they headed in the direction opposite the jail.

"We have one more stop," he grinned slyly, watching his partner trail behind him in the second squad car.

Evelyn was fuming. She had an idea why she was being arrested but she still didn't want to fully accept it. It was her own niece who had her arrested.

When they pulled into Angelica's driveway, Evelyn's stomach did a flip-flop. While Evelyn lived in a decent neighborhood, Angelica's was much more lavish; everybody who was anybody lived near her.

Evelyn lay on her side on the leather seat to be sure no one could see her as Angelica's arrest was happening. The officers weren't in the house more than five minutes before they emerged with Angelica, her hands behind her back, being guided to the second squad car.

Christie had a huge lump in her throat and, no matter how many times she swallowed it wouldn't go away. Her aunts had been arrested on criminal charges stemming from the theft of her father's money and property. She thought she'd feel vindicated but she felt terrible.

After Bill and Grace explained how the arrest happened Christie asked, "What's next? Will they go straight to jail? Will there be a trial?"

Bill talked quickly, "First we go before a judge and he determines whether there is enough evidence for criminal charges. But, Christie, I want you to know there is a possibility of the criminal charges being dismissed."

"What do you mean?" They had worked hard to have her aunts arrested so they could start getting answers but now Bill was saying the charges might be dropped?

Grace and jumped into the conversation, "Christie, we have solid evidence. Bill and I told you we believe we will get a judge to rule in our favor. Now whether it will be on criminal or civil charges we can't say for sure. If you want to see them locked up, the criminal charges are our best bet. If you want to force them to pay everything back, that would mean pursuing civil charges."

Christie hadn't even entertained the thought of sending her aunts to jail. She just wanted them to admit to stealing and pay it all back. She wanted them to do what was right by their brother.

"So what are the chances they will get the criminal charges dropped?"

Neither attorney spoke for a few seconds before Grace answered, "We can prepare for the charges being dropped and begin drawing up the civil papers now. I think their attorneys will push to drop the criminal charges and if that happens we can immediately serve them with papers for the civil lawsuit."

Christie just wanted this taken care of quickly. The last thing she wanted was to spend the next few months worrying about this case instead of concentrating on her family and work. "That works for me."

She wondered, with all that was happening, if her aunts felt any remorse.

"I can't believe that little brat," Evelyn said as she massaged her wrists and shaded her eyes from the bright sunshine.

Angelica ignored her sister and focused on finding the car Michael was supposed to be pulling to the front of the jail.

The sisters had spent a total of eight hours in jail and it had been uneventful. It was a different scenery than they'd experienced when they were arrested.

"Do you need us to take you home?" Angelica asked as Michael drove up.

Evelyn nodded and quickly jumped into the back seat of the sedan.

"We need to call our attorneys right now. Michael, you said you already communicated with them this morning?" Evelyn rambled as she looked out the window.

Michael nodded, "Mr. Sykes said he's pretty certain he can get these charges dropped immediately. They don't have enough evidence to convict you on the criminal charges. He's worried, though, that Christie will try to sue you in civil court. He wants y'all to be aware of that."

Angelica was speechless. She couldn't believe any of this was happening to her. "I just can't believe Christie. Why would she do this? Why would she go this far? She has to be stopped," she finally said as her voice cracked.

Not only was her niece messing with her good name, she was messing with her money.

"Maybe we should file charges against her as well. Who paid for the funeral? Who paid for Kenneth's hospital bills? Us." Evelyn said to no one in particular.

"Those aren't criminal charges," Michael said blandly. He knew what Evelyn was trying to do but she wasn't thinking rationally.

"Well, you know what I mean. Maybe there's something we can do to beat her at her own game."

"Maybe y'all should just let this die down. It's going to, you know," Michael reassured them as his own mind wandered to the secrets that Christie held against him.

"Are you kidding me, Michael? This child had us arrested, embarrassed and humiliated and you want us to let this die down? No, I say we fight fire with fire."

Michael looked over at a defeated Angelica and then back to the road. Technically, this wasn't his battle.

When they pulled into Evelyn's, a black Dodge Charger was already in the driveway. At the doorstep, a young, attractive blonde stood in a dark suit and glasses that framed her face.

"Are you Evelyn Robinson?" the girl asked sweetly as Angelica rolled down her window to take a closer look.

"Are you here to arrest me? If so, I'm not her," Evelyn replied with plenty of attitude.

"No, I'm not here to arrest you," the blonde laughed.

Evelyn found nothing funny about her day in jail and cleared her throat to let the woman know she could proceed.

"You've been served," the woman said as she handed a packet of papers to Evelyn and headed back to her car.

"Angelica, I've been served. How much better could this day get?"

The woman looked up. "Are you her sister, Angelica?"

Without realizing what she was doing, Angelica nodded her head.

"You've been served as well. I was just heading to your house. Glad I can kill two birds with one stone," the woman said as she handed Angelica a second packet and got in her car.

The sisters stood frozen with disbelief. Things couldn't get any worse for them.

Until they did.

Twenty Two

"You sure you're doing okay?" Anthony asked as he parked at the courthouse.

Christie had waited months for this moment; she was more ready than she could ever imagine. Even though the judge had decided to drop the criminal charges of theft, Christie was still able to sue in civil court. Christie thought she would feel defeated, knowing her aunts had gotten away from any criminal charges, but she just wanted justice in any form she could get it.

"I'm ready for this to start so it can be all over," Christie replied as she checked her makeup in the mirror. Her face seemed to be growing by the day. She'd watched as her nose spread halfway across her face and her eyes seemed to get lost in the chunkiness of her cheeks, but she didn't care. Her aunts were standing trial for stealing from her father and nothing could ruin that joy. "Let's go. I don't want to be late."

Christie wasn't sure what to expect when she arrived at the courthouse. She knew there had been some local news coverage of the case so she wondered if reporters would be camped out like she'd seen in the movies or if the building would be totally empty.

When they arrived at their designated courtroom, Christie was shocked to see a few family members sitting behind the defendant's side. Bill and Grace were at the prosecutors' table and waved her over.

"Anthony, why don't you have a seat behind us? Christie, everything should be starting soon," Grace said softly.

Since they had met the day before to go over what to expect, Christie wasn't nervous at all.

While Bill and Grace made small talk with Christie, a number of people came into the courtroom. Some people Christie knew and others were complete strangers.

"Some of those people are probably reporters. Just keep your poker face on like we talked about yesterday," Bill said as he kept his eye on the door.

Christie turned to look over her shoulder just as both her aunts entered the courtroom. Angelica seemed to glance at her for a half second before retreating to her table while Evelyn might have been walking a runway in Milan with how she strutted into the room.

"She's so extra," Christie said as she turned in her seat and placed her hand on the charm around her neck. The silver necklace and matching heart charm had been in Christie's possession since she was thirteen.

Her father had surprised her with a father-daughter day, treating her to lunch and the movies. As the two of them sat in her mother's driveway laughing about all they'd done and how much fun they'd had, her father pulled out a small box and handed it to her.

"I know you're growing up, Christie," her father began as she lifted the lid, "but I want you to know that you'll always be my baby girl whether I'm here or not and whether you're young or old. You'll always be my baby girl."

Christie gasped at the necklace. "Daddy, it's so pretty. Thank you," she said as she leaned over and kissed her father on the cheek.

From that moment on, whenever Christie was facing difficulty she wore that necklace. Her mother had even dubbed it her "lucky charm necklace" because it seemingly always brought her unexpected good luck.

Christie ran her finger over the necklace once again as her eyes went over to where her aunts and their lawyers sat. Angelica wore a dark red suit with a polka-dotted scarf and black heels while Aunt Evelyn was in a smoke gray pantsuit with black heels. Both women had their hair off their faces and were sporting glasses. If she didn't know everything they'd done, she would have been inclined to believe they were innocent just based on their looks. But she knew better. She knew all the facts and she knew all the years her father had worked to build up a nest egg. She also knew the tears she'd cried when she realized her own family had done the unthinkable.

Looking at her aunts was like watching a car accident—she couldn't turn away yet she couldn't bear to keep looking at them. She wanted to hate them.

Her mind told her she should but she couldn't force it. She loved them because of who they were; she was angry with them because of what they had done. Here they were—dressed like school teachers—and all Christie could feel for them was pity. Their lawyer wasn't too shabby either. In fact, Christie thought as she took a closer look at him, she knew him. Thomas Sykes was one of the most well-known attorneys in the nation. Christie glanced over at Grace and Bill and hoped they were just as powerful. Thomas Sykes had handled media mogul Suzanne Winter's high-profile case and won the trial with rave reviews.

Christie said a silent prayer and turned back to face the judge's bench.

"Babe," Anthony whispered, leaning forward, "Junior just walked in."

Christie's heart stopped. She and Junior had become closer than ever so she wondered where he would choose to sit. Christie glanced at him before quickly turning to face forward. Watching from the corner of her eye, Christie saw Junior go over and speak to a few family members while hugging his mother. A part of her wanted to scream. If he wanted to support his mother by sitting on her side, Christie couldn't let that affect her. Still, she'd feel betrayed because of everything she'd confided to Junior about the case.

It wasn't until she felt two strong hands on her shoulders that she turned around.

"Hey, Chris," Junior said.

"Hey," Christie grinned as she stood up and embraced her cousin tightly.

"Are you doing okay?" Junior asked returning her hug.

"You know what? I am...I really am," Christie said as they stepped apart.

"Junior, you don't have to sit on my side if you don't want to. I know that's your mother and—"

Junior held a finger to his lips. "They're going to be mad, Chris. I don't care," he said as he sat next to Anthony.

Christie looked over at Evelyn and Angelica while the rest of the family watched.

"Junior!" Angelica said sternly from across the aisle.

Christie's side of the courtroom stared across the aisle in what felt like a face-down. Angelica looked more hurt than shocked while Evelyn looked like she could spit fire.

"Junior, I am your mother," Angelica said, her voice rattled. Michael reached for her arm but she quickly snatched it away. Christie had seen her aunt get emotional but never to this magnitude.

Junior dropped his head and tried to tune them out. A few people were talking but nearly everyone silently observed the scene unfolding in front of them.

"Junior, do you hear me?" Angelica was cracking. Christie knew that Angelica would be the first to break down. Evelyn seemed to have less of a heart and it was showing.

"Angelica, you need to calm down," Evelyn quietly said as she tried her best not to look in Christie and Junior's direction.

"Mom stop. Right is right and wrong is wrong. I'm sitting here not because I don't love you but because I'm standing up for what's right. Regardless of how this plays out, I want to be able to sleep at night knowing I stood behind what I believed," Junior finally said loudly, silencing the entire courtroom.

Angelica was at a loss for words. Her own son had called her out. Devastation swept over her face as she tried to keep the tears from falling.

"After everything your mother has done for you? How dare you turn your back on her like this?" Evelyn spoke up as she pointed in Junior's direction.

Junior had finally had enough. "Don't *you* tell me anything about sacrifice or turning my back on anyone, Aunt Evelyn. You don't think I know everything? I do."

Christie wanted to intervene and calm her cousin down, but she couldn't. She knew he needed to speak the things he was saying as much as they needed to hear it from him.

"I know everything. How could you?" cried Junior, tears streaming down his face.

Angelica opened her mouth to respond but the bailiff spoke before she could.

"The Honorable Judge Fernandez is presiding over this trial. Order in the court. Everyone quiet down," he said firmly.

Christie looked over at her aunts before taking her seat. The shock on all of their faces made Christie smile. Though that part of her family had disowned her, Christie had all the family she needed on her side.

"Quiet down! Quiet down!" the judge said as she appeared and took her seat. She was a beautiful older Hispanic woman who had dark hair with a large gray streak in the middle.

Mr. Sykes stood to speak first. "Your Honor, I have a motion to dismiss all civil charges. My clients are well-known women in the community and have no idea how Mrs. Adams' charges relate to them. They have no recollection of a bank account nor do they know anything about Mr. Whitfield's missing money and personal property. This is all a waste of the court's time, Your Honor."

Looking at her aunts, Christie cringed. They hadn't been in the court for five minutes and were already trying to lie their way out of trouble. Her heart was heavy. She had hoped they would be truthful, get everything out in the open and at least admit to their wrongs. Christie saw now that this was going to be harder than she expected.

Judge Fernandez seemed humored by the fast-talking Mr. Sykes. Dressed in his flashy suit and fancy shoes, Mr. Sykes looked more like a walking infomercial than a defense attorney.

"Mr. Sykes, up to the same old tricks, I see," she said with a smirk. "I've read over these charges and all of the evidence and the civil charges will remain. Anything else?"

The judge was talking, but Christie couldn't take her eyes off the women she'd grown up admiring. Christie remembered days when she would emulate the way her Aunt Angelica walked and talked and how she would try to be as cool and laid-back as her Aunt Evelyn. She knew they were aware she was staring but they diverted their eyes.

Finally, Angelica looked down at the floor then up at Christie.

All Christie could do was look at her aunt with pity and shake her head. Her eyes were pleading for answers but her heart was shaken from the shock of everything.

"Why?" Christie mouthed. Her eyes were filling with tears and she wanted her aunt to know that she, too, had emotions and feelings. She, too, was hurt by how everything had happened. She, too, had lost more than money; she'd lost her family.

Angelica continued to stare for a few moments before taking a deep breath and looking away.

"Ladies and gentleman of the court, I'd like you to understand one thing. Christie Whitfield-Adams does not care about money," Bill Spectrum said to start his opening argument. "You see, all of her life Christie has grown up working for everything she had. Along the way, she always had two constant figures in her life: her mother and her father."

Christie glanced over her shoulder at her mother and smiled. She was happy. Alise missed the blow-up between Angelica and Junior but made it in time for the opening arguments.

"Only one of those constant figures is here today. When Christie's father, Kenneth, became ill last year no one was quicker to be at his side than his only daughter. She spent countless nights at the hospital to make sure her father—one of the people who pushed her to be the person she is—had the best of care. Sadly after her father passed away, Christie was met with more devastating news—someone had been stealing from her father as he was dying."

Bill paused to let the words sink in.

"Someone had been stealing everything Kenneth had saved, everything he worked for all his life, while he lay facing death in a hospital bed."

Christie felt her bottom lip begin to quiver. She knew the facts of the case, but it still hurt to hear.

"Kenneth was a saver, by nature. He was the type of person who would save a penny or a dollar. 'Every little bit helps,' he would always tell Christie. So imagine Christie's surprise when his bank informed her that Kenneth's account had been cleaned out to the tune of $1.5 million. Every bit of Kenneth's money, and some personal belongings, were gone almost immediately after he was."

Bill's voice rose as he continued, "It would be one thing if the money had been stolen by a stranger, but the only people with access to Kenneth's bank account were his sisters." Bill pointed in the direction of Evelyn and Angelica.

"This case is going to reveal exactly how Kenneth's own sisters conspired to steal from their dying brother in a twisted scheme that left their family in shambles. From mystery bank accounts to tie-ins with others, we have no doubt that we know what happened to Kenneth's money."

Christie lowered her head as Bill kept speaking.

"Christie deserves justice. Not for the money but because her father deserved better than this. This family is not torn apart because of Christie's desire for $1.5 million but because Christie stood up for her father when he was no longer alive to do it for himself."

Christie noticed the judge looking in her direction as she scribbled notes.

"What could be worse? Having your family spit in your face or having your family spit in your face and lie about it? Christie Whitfield-Adams wants answers and by the end of this trial, you're going to understand exactly why Evelyn and Angelica should be found guilty. That's all, Your Honor."

Junior and Anthony both reached forward and placed a hand on Christie's shoulder. Their support was nice, but Christie felt more alone than ever. Hearing Bill's opening argument made her aware of just how bad her situation was. She held her lucky charm and swallowed the lump in her throat.

She needed to keep her tunnel vision on or she was going to be run over. She was done letting people walk all over her. She meant business now.

Twenty Three

Christie fished nervously through her soup for nothing in particular. She knew she needed to eat but she didn't have much of an appetite.

"Babe, you know we have to be back to the courthouse in thirty minutes—your food is going to get cold," Anthony said as he munched on his burger.

For a second, Christie wondered what it would feel like to be carefree. She knew Anthony was in this with her, but he wasn't in her shoes. He knew the tears she cried but he wasn't the one crying them. He knew how hurt she was but he wasn't the one in pain.

The past few days in court had been rough, to say the least. From her aunts lying about their knowledge of the missing money to their blatant disrespect for Christie and her father in their statements, Christie was teetering between being livid and being depressed.

"What do you think they meant when they said they *knew* I was up to no good when I went to visit my father?" Christie asked as she stared off into space.

Earlier in the day, Angelica had taken the stand and rocked the courtroom with her insinuations. They were still on Christie's mind.

"Ms. Harrison, you've made it pretty clear that you are completely clueless as to why your niece—your brother's only daughter—would accuse you and your sister of stealing his money, correct?" Grace Humphries drilled Angelica who sat with an emotionless look on her face.

"That's correct," Angelica said as she kept her eyes on Grace. Christie wondered if Grace was tough enough to handle her aunt.

"Great. So explain to the court why, in your mind, she would make up this story about the missing money." Grace folded her arms in a relaxed manner and motioned for Angelica to answer her question.

Angelica looked like she was scrambling for an answer as her eyes darted from her attorney to Grace.

"Why wouldn't she? It's no secret that Mrs. Adams and my sister Evelyn have never gotten along. This might just be some big plot to get revenge on the both of us."

Grace chuckled. "So you're telling me Christie has made up this elaborate story, going through the trouble of creating evidence to support it, all because she wants revenge on you and your sister? Explain to me why she might want this revenge."

Inside Christie was laughing hysterically. No one ever talked that way to Angelica and she knew it must be tearing her up not to go all the way off on Grace.

"I…I don't know exactly, but I do know every time she came to see her father in the hospital she was always up to no good. From picking fights with me and my sister to turning her father against us, it was clear that she was the one who had ulterior motives," Angelica shot back.

Christie was appalled at what her aunt was implying. Was she preparing to say that Christie was after her father's money? Christie squirmed in frustration and cleared her throat to let Grace know she was in disagreement.

Grace nodded and changed her line of questioning.

"Ms. Harrison, did you hold the Power of Attorney over your brother's account?"

Christie grinned. She knew the answer and Angelica knew the answer as well; it was damning.

"You know my sister and I both did. You're the smart lawyer, right?" Angelica said through gritted teeth.

"Ms. Harrison, all you need to do is answer the question. Any slick talk can wait," Judge Fernandez stated without looking up.

"Yes, I did," Angelica finally said.

It was the golden answer the prosecutors had been waiting for. The admission felt like heaven to Christie who sat back in her chair and exhaled. She knew they were nowhere near the finish line, but they were closer than they'd ever been before. Now all she needed was for her aunts to continue telling the truth. Little did she know the tricks they had up their sleeve that would throw her a killer curve.

Christie sat quietly in her hard chair and watched Mr. Sykes argue that his clients had no knowledge on the whereabouts of the stolen money. He called witness after witness who vouched that these women weren't thieves and that Christie had always been "a trouble-maker." Some of them Christie knew and others were complete strangers.

The line of questioning bored Christie. Mr. Sykes asked the same questions over and over until he received the perfect answer and most often that answer was a lie.

By the middle of the trial, the only thing keeping Christie sane and pushing forward were thoughts of her father. She inhaled and strangely found herself smelling her father's signature Yves Saint Laurent cologne. She searched the room and tried to locate the source of the smell. After a few seconds, Christie chalked it up to her nose playing tricks on her. Until she smelled it again.

"Do you smell Yves Saint Laurent cologne?" Christie whispered quietly into Grace's ear. Grace chuckled and shook her head before returning her attention to Mr. Sykes.

The scent of her father took her far from the courtroom and her present situation as she began daydreaming about one of the last in-person conversations she had him. Ironically, Kenneth had been wearing Yves Saint Laurent cologne when they had the conversation.

"Daddy, I brought your cologne up here. I thought it'd make you feel better," Christie said as she kissed her father's forehead. He was weaker than she'd ever seen him and it broke her heart into a million and one pieces.

She had dealt with the probability that her father was terminally ill but she wasn't ready to give up without a strong fight for his life.

"Baby girl…" Kenneth said in a raspy, weak voice as he widened his eyes.

"Yes, Daddy?"

"Sit down. We need to talk."

Christie sat in the uncomfortably oversized chair next to her father's bed. For some reason, she was nervous. Her father didn't have a joking look on his face and nothing about him said he was in the mood to play.

"Christie, I need you to be sure everything in my will is followed exactly. I mean everything. I've laid it all out and it's in my safe deposit box at the bank."

This wasn't what she wanted to hear. She wanted her father to tell her something funny that would make her laugh until her stomach hurt. She didn't want to hear him talk about wills and death.

"But, Daddy—"

"Baby girl, I know this isn't something you want to deal with, but you're my child. When I'm…when I'm gone…you're going to be the only voice able to speak for me. I need to make sure you know how important it is to me that you follow every instruction in my will."

Christie's eyes filled with tears.

"Okay, Daddy."

Kenneth cleared his throat and reached for the jug of water in front of him before taking a sip. "This is no time for tears, baby girl. These are my last wishes and I know there may be some people who think they know what I want better than I do. My last will and Testament is exactly what I want. Don't let anyone do anything differently."

Christie had never heard her father speak so adamantly about anything.

"I've left everything to you, baby girl. Make sure the rest of the family is taken care of if by chance they are in need. You're my only child, Christie," her father finished as his voice choked, "and I know you'll respect my wishes."

Without warning, Christie started crying. For the first time she realized that her father knew his time was drawing to a close and it hurt.

She had repeated that story countless times to Bill and Grace, making sure she didn't leave out a single solitary word. It was imperative, Bill said, that she didn't.

"Your Honor, we'd like to call Deborah Matthews to the stand," Mr. Sykes said, snapping Christie out of her daydream.

Christie turned to see Deborah walk into the courtroom in a dark blazer and skirt. She had on a striped shirt and looked more professional than Christie had ever seen her. Christie wondered why Deborah was testifying for her aunts when she didn't trust them and they didn't trust her.

"Please state your name," Mr. Sykes said as he walked to the prosecution table.

"Deborah Matthews."

"Thank you. What was your relation to Mr. Whitfield?"

"I was his fiancée."

"I'm sorry about your loss, Ms. Matthews. Tell me, how many conversations did you have with Mr. Whitfield about his final wishes and his will?"

Deborah took a sip of water before answering, "I had several conversations with Kenny about that."

Kenny? No one called her father Kenny, not even his closest friends. Christie had a bad feeling.

"Please tell the court what these conversations consisted of and what Mr. Whitfield said he wanted done with his estate upon his death."

Christie leaned forward and listened closely to what Deborah would say.

"Kenny said he wanted to leave everything to his sisters and to me. He did want Christie to have some of his money and belongings, but he said he knew she would be okay without it. He wanted his sisters and I to divvy up his belongings and money, pay off any of his remaining bills, and live comfortably with the rest."

Christie heard herself scream, "LIAR!"

It was the first time she'd had an outburst and it was like an out-of-body experience.

"Counselor, please control your client. I will not tolerate outbursts in my courtroom," Judge Fernandez said sternly.

Christie covered her mouth as she took deep breaths and tried to calm herself down. Her face was hot and she was livid.

Turning around, she looked back at her mother, Junior and Anthony in shock. Deborah was essentially calling *her* a liar.

"Ms. Matthews, are you telling the court that Mr. Whitfield made no mention of his daughter getting his money and belongings as she claims in her deposition?"

Deborah nodded and did her best to avoid the dumbfounded look on Christie's face. "That's correct. Kenny said he had taken care of Christie and she was married now. We were planning our entire life together and he wanted to make sure I was still able to do those things—even if it was without him."

Christie gasped as she listened to Deborah negate everything she knew her father stood for. Kenneth was a family man and as he'd said over and over again, Christie was his sole concern whether she was married or not.

Why was Deborah lying? Why was she painting Christie to be after her father's money? What happened to the nice woman her father described and with whom she'd had lunch?

"Last question, Ms. Matthews. Do you think Evelyn and Angelica had anything to do with the missing money or possessions?"

Deborah wasted no time in replying, "I think it's impossible. And foolish to imagine that his own sisters, who took care of him on his deathbed and sacrificed so much for him, would steal from him. So, no, I don't think they had anything to do with it. I think this is all because Christie misses her father and is trying to do whatever she can to hold on to his memory."

If she had any question before, Christie was now aware that Deborah didn't mean her father any good.

"I need a break. I can't breathe. Please ask for a recess. Fifteen minutes. Please," Christie begged as she leaned forward on the table and gasped for air.

Grace stood up, requested a recess and was surprised when Judge Fernandez agreed.

Christie pushed through the courtroom doors inhaling and exhaling as if they were the last breaths she would ever take. The sun was shining brightly and it was one of the most beautiful days in a long time. But Christie found it hard to see any of the beauty because of all the lies she'd just heard.

Pulling out her cell phone, Christie punched in a few numbers and pressed the phone to her ear. "I need a favor, a huge favor, I need your help," she said to the person on the other end.

She wasn't taking their lies lying down.

Twenty Four

"Calm down and stop fidgeting," Alise said to Christie as they entered the courtroom. Christie found herself rolling her eyes as she tried her best to ignore her mother. It was easier for Alise to tell Christie to calm down than for Christie to actually do it.

Alise had been in court every day with her daughter and Christie was beyond grateful. In addition to being by her daughter's side during the trial, she had also traveled back and forth between her home in Chicago and Indianapolis to help Christie and Anthony out when needed.

"I'm calm, Ma," Christie lied.

The wooden courtroom door looked duller than ever. Christie was never happy to enter the courtroom but today it caused a dull ache in the bottom of her stomach that made her cringe.

"If you say so," Alise said as she looked over at Anthony and shrugged.

When they entered the courtroom a few people were buzzing around preparing for the day's trial. Christie ignored them all and headed to her familiar seat.

"Do you remember all the answers Bill and Grace talked to you about?" Anthony whispered as he leaned forward and rubbed his wife's back.

She was irritable beyond belief and even Anthony's touch couldn't calm her.

"Babe, I don't need to remember any answers. I'm telling the truth."

"Christie, they know what they're doing and since today is the day that Sykes questions you on the stand, it might be best to at least remember *some* of the responses they discussed with you," Anthony said with finality in his voice.

He was right. Christie had been so amped up on emotion it made her think irrationally. According to Bill and Grace they had a slam-dunk case. But after Mr. Sykes started presenting and questioning witnesses, Christie wondered if that prediction was still accurate.

"Okay, I'll remember," Christie said as the courtroom filled.

It seemed that as the days went by more and more people were attending the trial. Maybe it was because Christie was a well-known figure or maybe it was because people identified with betrayal—there was no way to know.

Bill and Grace sat down at the table as Grace slid a cup of coffee towards Christie.

"Thank you," Christie said wrapping her hands around the warm cup.

"Are you ready for today?" Bill inquired as he flipped through a notepad.

Christie nodded and forced herself to look at her lawyers. In these two strangers, lay the fate of her father's last wishes and the outcome of her family's division. Christie wondered if Bill and Grace knew how much was at stake.

As if on cue, Grace turned and looked at Christie. "You'll do fine. Just remember everything we told you and never let them see you sweat."

Nodding again, Christie reached for her bottle of water and took a swig.

Gone were her days of feeling sad for herself and her situation; now Christie just wanted justice and she wanted it swiftly.

Grace continued talking to Christie about how Mr. Sykes would probably try to get a reaction from her as Evelyn, Angelica and their legal team entered the room.

Christie watched them come in with grins on their faces and wondered what that was all about. She watched her aunts' body language and narrowed her eyes at their smirks. If she wasn't mistaken, they seemed to be gloating. Besides being irritated, bothered and tired, Christie was now ticked off.

"Why are they grinning like Cheshire cats? Like they just found out they're innocent?" Christie asked, interrupting Grace.

Both attorneys turned to look and shook their heads.

"It's just a scare tactic I've seen Mr. Sykes use it over and over again, Christie. If he can make you appear to be an emotionally unstable daughter who only filed this suit because she is bitter, they'll have a better shot of walking out of here innocent," Grace replied.

Staring over at her aunts Christie found herself grimacing. Aunt Angelica was wearing a black wrap-dress that stopped at her knees with a pair of nude pumps while Evelyn had on a cream pantsuit with black pumps. During the entire trial, they'd dressed as if they were posing for twin-themed Glamour Shots.

"Don't focus on them and their tactics. Block it out. We've got a slam-dunk case," Bill reminded her.

Christie was tired of hearing that term because as she'd seen, Mr. Sykes was playing hardball and she knew some jurors were being swayed.

Junior walked into the courtroom and took his usual seat beside Alise. Christie smiled. Even if the trial had removed all of the negative family from her life, it had drawn her closer to the genuine members. No longer did Christie see the need for a big family; she was content with a small circle with truthful hearts.

"Ladies and gentlemen, let's get started," Judge Fernandez said as she banged her gavel, snapping Christie to attention.

"Mr. Sykes," Judge Fernandez said, "I believe you have the floor."

Mr. Sykes stood up, buttoned the jacket of his obviously expensive suit and smiled in the judge's direction.

"Thank you, Your Honor. We'd like to call Christie Whitfield-Adams to the stand."

Christie had pictured this moment in her head a thousand times before. What would people say as she walked to the stand? How would she look? Would she be able to keep it together?

As it turned out, Christie walked so quickly to the stand that she didn't even remember the walk, the stares or the need to care.

"Mrs. Adams, I won't waste your time because I know you have a lot going on right now. I just have a few questions for you," Mr. Sykes said as he walked slowly towards the stand. Christie could hear his shoes clicking on the ground.

"Mrs. Adams—may I call you Christie?"

"Sure."

"Thank you. Christie, please tell the court about the last conversation you had with your father regarding his will."

Christie remembered the conversation like it was a tattoo on her forehead. She couldn't forget her father's words and tone if she wanted to.

"My father told me to make sure I did everything in his will, which was located at his bank in a safety deposit box, exactly as it was spelled out."

"And you're sure you had this conversation with him, correct?"

Christie had only interacted with Mr. Sykes a few times but she knew he was nothing more than a condescending jerk. She couldn't stand him.

"Yes, sir. There's probably no other conversation I ever had with my father that sticks with me more. He was never as adamant about anything as he was about all of his wishes being respected," Christie said as she gritted her teeth and looked over at Bill and Grace who were watching with pleased looks on their faces.

"Okay. Now, you have met Ms. Matthews before, correct?"

"Yes, I have."

"And what was her relation to your father?"

"She was his girlfriend…or fiancée."

Mr. Sykes turned to the side and stared at Christie for a few seconds before speaking again.

"Is it fair to say that you're in a happy marriage, Christie?"

Christie felt her face getting hot. This was the reaction Mr. Sykes wanted and Christie was trying her best not to give it to him.

"Excuse me? What does my marriage have to do with this case?"

Mr. Sykes cleared his throat and looked up to the judge for assistance.

"Mrs. Adams, please just answer his question."

"Fine. Yes, I'm in a happy marriage."

"And would you say that everything you and your husband run by each other holds more weight than what you run by others?" Mr. Sykes asked with a chuckle.

"I don't understand the question," Christie said, remembering Bill and Grace's suggestion of having him rephrase, and possibly shift the perception of, his question.

Mr. Sykes plastered a phony smile on his face, turned back to Christie and asked his question again.

"Would you want people to believe what your husband says are your last wishes or what someone else says?"

Christie's heart stopped. Obviously, she would want someone to listen to Anthony. He would know her best, but this was different. Still, she was only being given one opportunity to answer so it had to be correct.

"I would want someone to listen to my *husband*, yes," Christie said as she shot daggers toward Mr. Sykes and then toward her aunts.

Mr. Sykes put his hands together and smiled as he paced in front of the stand. Christie knew the point he was making and she was ready for her rebuttal.

"So, knowing that Ms. Matthews was your father's fiancée, not his girlfriend as you stated earlier, why would you think her testimony shouldn't trump yours? You are saying different things, right?"

"Mr. Sykes, my father and Ms. Matthews were *not* husband and wife. They were engaged. My father updated his will a few months before he fell ill. He was dating Ms. Matthews so if he wanted her as a beneficiary I'm sure he would have made that change then. But to answer your question, I'm his daughter and I'm the only person my father trusted to handle his affairs if something were to happen to him. That's why my testimony should trump that of Ms. Matthews."

Mr. Sykes' face looked flustered. Christie could tell he had expected her to lose her cool but she hadn't.

Christie kept watching the door, hoping that Janice would appear. She held the key to the biggest discovery of the case.

After hearing Deborah's testimony, Christie knew something wasn't right. Everything Deborah had once said had changed and she seemed extra suspicious.

Acting on impulse, Christie had called Janice for a favor.

"I need you to look into what's going on with the Tyson Hospice Center, my aunts and Deborah Matthews. See if there has been any large deposits made or something, if you can," Christie had said a few days earlier standing on the court steps and trying to catch her breath.

Janice had always been able to discover secrets. The question was, despite Christie's suspicions, were there any secrets to discover? There had been more twists and turns in the case than Christie had expected, so she was hoping Janice would come through.

Mr. Sykes walked directly in front of Christie on the stand and cleared his throat. "Christie, is it true that your finances are in a bit of distress right now?"

Her heart stopped. In the past she and Anthony had encountered a few financial issues that not only threatened their financial well-being but also their relationship. Christie had always been good with money but as she started making more, she somehow made a mess of her finances. It wasn't until she was four years out of college and working that Christie and Anthony recognized there was an issue because they were both well paid but barely getting by. The realization that Christie's credit card debt was the culprit had rocked their relationship and almost led Anthony to ask for a divorce. But they worked through it and were well down the path to better finances.

"No, that's incorrect," Christie said as she felt tears creeping up on her.

"Did you all once have financial issues?" Mr. Sykes asked again. He was adamant about getting an answer.

Christie took a deep breath and closed her eyes. "Yes, a few years ago."

"So is this all an attempt to collect money to fix those issues? Is that what this entire sham of a case is about, Christie?"

Christie felt like someone had punched her in the gut and was standing over her laughing. She wanted to retaliate, but she didn't have it in her.

Looking up at Mr. Sykes, she opened her mouth to respond but nothing came out.

Just then she saw the door swing open and Janice rushed toward Bill and Grace. The three of them huddled together while everyone stared in suspense. It was like something out of a movie Christie thought and she was on the edge of her seat to know what was going on.

Bill grinned wide enough for Christie to see all of his teeth and her heart jumped with joy, though she wasn't sure why.

"Your Honor, we need to request an immediate brief recess."

"On what grounds, counselor?" Judge Fernandez asked as she pulled her glasses from her face.

Grace couldn't stop smiling as she replied, "We have brand new evidence and we must review it immediately."

Christie sat up in her chair and heard Judge Fernandez grant the recess. Before the room could clear out Christie spoke loudly, "I want to answer your question, Mr. Sykes."

As the room grew quiet she said, "No, this lawsuit isn't a reason to get money or to lessen my financial burden. My father raised me to be self-sufficient and I've never asked anyone for any help or money to fix what I did wrong. Did we have financial issues? Yes. Are we considering using my father's money for that? No. I have a family and the only thing I'm concerned about is making sure my family never ends up like the one that betrayed my father."

Christie stepped down from the stand and walked slowly towards her table. This time though she was paying attention to the stares, the whispers and the eye-rolls from the other side of the room and none of it mattered.

What did matter rested in a thick manila envelope in Janice's hand. Christie couldn't wait to tear it open.

Twenty Five

Christie rocked slowly in the oversized rocking chair as her feet barely touched the ground. Finally, she was content.

"Do you need anything?" she heard Anthony yell from the next room. She wanted to answer, but didn't. All she could do was look down and smile.

Seconds later, Anthony entered the room with a wide grin on his face.

"I'm going to take that as a no, babe," he laughed as he slowly approached her.

Christie looked up and smiled until her cheeks hurt. Anthony's face had never looked as beautiful as it did today and she knew exactly why.

It had been three weeks since she'd left the courtroom, where she'd spent nearly a month, for good. The trial had gone well at first and had slowly blossomed into going great.

After Janice rushed into the courtroom with the mystery envelope, the entire room had fallen silent in anticipation.

"The contents of this envelope prove that Angelica Harrison and Evelyn Robinson bought off Deborah Matthews and her family, who own the Tyson Hospice Center," Janice said when they were finally in a private room. Christie glanced over at Grace and Bill and raised her eyebrows.

"Are you serious?" Christie asked, knowing Janice had never lied to her before.

"As a heart attack," Janice shot back.

It was true, Bill and Grace confirmed. The information Janice had found verified that a huge payment had been deposited into Deborah's account then funneled into the account of Tyson Hospice. The complication was in proving exactly why the payment was made. While it was obvious to Christie, she knew they would need a rock-solid explanation in order to convince the judge.

"If we introduce this, we'll risk having them discredit it. If we don't have a solid explanation, it could be tossed out," Grace said as she took her seat.

Christie thought long and hard. She knew as soon as they introduced the information her aunts' attorneys would have a quick explanation.

Between Janice and her attorneys, Christie couldn't hear herself think so she finally made an executive decision.

"Let's use it," she said quietly as everyone in the room stared at her.

"Are you sure? This could—" Grace started before Christie held up her finger.

"We have a strong case without this, but I think this is the piece we were waiting for. I know we're taking a chance that it will be thrown out but at this point I think it's worth the risk. We all know the truth and now this evidence helps us *show* it so if it gets thrown out, Evelyn and Angelica will still know that we know."

It was drastic and Christie knew it, but she had to go with her gut. Her heart was telling her it was the right move, but her nerves were trying their best to make her think differently.

"Well, there you have it. Give me and Grace a few minutes to strategize on how to present this and we'll go back in," Bill said with a wink.

Christie could tell he agreed with her decision and she was grateful.

"Your Honor, I understand this is last minute," Bill said as he straightened his tie once they all returned to the courtroom, "but we'd like to bring Evelyn Robinson to the stand for questioning."

The courtroom buzzed as people tried to make sense of the left-field request from Christie's attorney. Christie shifted in her seat and glanced at her aunts. She took in the worry settling on their faces and for a split second wanted to call it all off. She knew her aunts had no idea what evidence she had up her sleeve. She also knew once it came out they would be ready to bolt. Grace tapped Christie on the shoulder to whisper in her ear and by the time she looked back her aunts were huddled frantically around their own attorneys.

Evelyn's walk to the stand was a quick one. Christie couldn't tell if she just wanted to get it over with, or if she was rushing to begin so she could set the record straight.

After the formalities, Bill went for blood.

"Ms. Robinson, do you agree with your sister when she says that you followed, to the best of your knowledge, your brother's last wishes exactly as he wanted them."

Evelyn swallowed and nodded before answering, "Yes, that is correct."

"Explain to me exactly what *you* understood your brother's last wishes to be."

Evelyn looked wide-eyed over Bill's shoulder toward her sister and her attorney. Christie turned and glanced back at Anthony, Junior and her mother to see if they saw the nervousness too. This was new. Christie had seen her aunt in all type of situations, but she'd never seen her panic stricken like this.

"I…uh…Kenneth wanted us to make sure everything was taken care of after he was gone. That's what we did."

"And when you say 'everything was taken care of' what and whom does that include?"

Evelyn's face turned white as she reached for the glass of water in front of her and slowly took a sip. Christie knew what that meant. The whole courtroom did—Evelyn was stalling.

"He wanted us to make sure his funeral, his medical bills, his house and his family were all taken care of," Evelyn said as she stared Bill square in his eyes.

Bill chuckled to himself, "Did his family solely include you and your sister Angelica, Ms. Robinson?"

Evelyn gasped as she clutched her chest and stared at the judge as if the questioning was out of line. Judge Fernandez looked back at Evelyn and nodded for her to answer.

After a few seconds, Evelyn's face was red and she was ready to tell Bill off; it was all in her eyes.

"My sister and I were the sole providers for my brother during the last few months of his life. His daughter came to visit a few times but day in and day out we were the ones who bore the brunt of the work. So, yes, we were the sole people he wanted to take care of after he passed away."

Christie felt her eyes water and her palms grow clammy. She felt sick to her stomach and just wanted to leave. Hearing her aunt flat-out lie to the courtroom made Christie cringe.

"So besides the doctors, hospital and funeral home, you and your sister were the only people who received compensation after Kenneth's death, correct?" Bill drilled.

Evelyn just nodded.

"That's interesting, Ms. Robinson," Bill said as he walked to the prosecution table, picked up the mystery envelope and proceeded toward the judge's bench, "because what I have here shows that Deborah Matthews and Tyson Hospice received well over $80,000 through a wire from you and your sister. What was this for?"

The room erupted in a series of gasps and shouts as everyone tried to make sense of what was happening.

Evelyn stood up and pointed at Bill but said nothing. Her eyes shot fire but her face showed confusion about how they could have uncovered information about the wire.

"Ms. Robinson, unless you want to be removed from this court, I advise you to sit down and answer his question," Judge Fernandez said sharply.

Christie glanced over to her Aunt Angelica and was shocked to see her attorney sitting back with an angry look on his face. It seemed they hadn't even informed their own team of the wire. It looked like this was the first time they were hearing about it.

Once the room calmed down, Christie focused her attention back on her Aunt Evelyn. Something in her had shifted. She was breathing heavier, her face was sweaty and it looked like she was seconds away from cracking. Still, Bill pressed on with his questioning.

"What was this wire for?" he repeated.

Evelyn looked at the floor then back at Bill. Her eyes were producing so many tears Christie couldn't understand how she could see straight. She opened her mouth, but nothing came out. Christie saw her aunt struggle to say something and she felt sympathetic for a split second before remembering her aunts had placed themselves in this deceitful predicament.

"I...I just...I'm sorry. Kenneth, I'm sorry..." Evelyn said in a whisper.

Christie heard her but wasn't sure she'd heard correctly.

"Please repeat what you just said, Ms. Robinson," Bill said as he approached her.

Evelyn looked up at him and stared. She looked lost and out of it. Still, it seemed she couldn't control what her mouth was saying.

"I'm just…I'm sorry. To my brother and my family, I just…" Evelyn said as she looked around the packed courtroom. Suddenly she jumped from her seat. "Everyone looks like…everyone looks like Kenneth!" Evelyn shouted as she stood up and started shaking her head uncontrollably.

Christie looked on with suspicion as her aunt appeared to have a nervous breakdown. She was shaking, her eyes were wide and she couldn't stop yelling, "I'm sorry! I'm sorry!"

When the bailiff was finally able to calm Evelyn down, Judge Fernandez called for a quick recess. Christie's heart was heavy but more than anything she was confused. Was her aunt now feeling remorse because they'd revealed the wire or would she have felt remorse anyway?

Once court resumed, Christie found it hard to take her eyes off the papers in front of her. She didn't want to look at her aunts and she didn't want to look at the judge. She just wanted the last few days of court to breeze by so she could hear the words she'd dreamed of hearing for months.

The last few days of the trial were predictable. Closing arguments from her aunts' attorney painted Christie as an ungrateful, money-hungry daughter who was more concerned with her father's finances than his health. Christie cringed as she heard herself being depicted in such a hateful light, but she knew the truth and that's all that mattered.

Remembering the last day in court before the verdict was announced Christie closed her eyes and sat back in the rocking chair as Anthony placed his hands on her tense shoulders.

It had been three weeks since the verdict but Christie was still smiling at how life had unfolded.

"You feel okay?" Anthony asked as he massaged her shoulders gently.

Christie nodded and looked up at him with a smile.

"We don't need you passing out again," Anthony joked, reminding her of the day of the verdict.

Christie giggled and shook her head. That morning was a blur. She had been up all of the night before, hadn't eaten much and was tired out of her mind. Still she got up, dressed and headed into court like nothing was wrong. But something *was* wrong. As Judge Fernandez asked the court to rise to hear the verdict, Christie felt her hands shake. Christie swallowed and stood up. She tried to focus but her vision was blurry.

"On the charges of civil theft…" the judge started just as Christie felt her knees go weak. Her body crumbled to the floor. Christie had passed out.

It wasn't until Christie woke up at the hospital that she even remembered she'd been in court.

"What…what happened, babe?" she asked Anthony. She was still in the black pantsuit she'd put on earlier that morning.

"Justice was served," Anthony said as he rubbed her hand.

Christie's eyes filled with tears. She wanted him to go more into detail but she was still playing with the words that danced in her ears.

"Justice was served," Christie repeated to herself.

She'd wanted to jump out of her skin and run around the hospital, but knew she couldn't. Besides, she reasoned, she hadn't pressed charges for any reason other than to be sure her father's wishes were carried out.

"And Angelica and Evelyn?" Christie asked, peering up at her husband.

"Of course they were shocked but the judge saw the truth and justice was served, honey."

Christie smiled as the hospital monitors beeped behind her, alerting her to her heartbeat. In that moment, Christie felt like her heart had been restored.

"There are a few reporters outside waiting to interview you. When you're feeling up to it, of course," Anthony said.

"Interview me? Why?"

Anthony chuckled and sat on the edge of her bed. "Your story resonated with others, babe. People can relate to being betrayed–especially by family members. They want to know there's a light at the end of the tunnel."

Christie had never thought about it like that. Through all the trials and tribulations of finding out that family and strangers were against her, Christie had never realized that others were watching and being inspired.

"I guess now's the time for you to think about releasing that memoir, babe," Anthony said with a wink.

Since her father's death, Christie had been journaling everything, including her thoughts on the situation, in hopes of turning it into a book. To her it was only to release some of her stress but now she knew there was a bigger purpose.

And just like that, her life had changed…almost overnight.

After the two reporters that were waiting to interview her in the hospital, there had been a slew of others. Christie obliged them all. It was, after all, great promotion for her plan to release her memoir. So there she sat, reflecting on how justice had been served. Her bad experience continued to create unbelievable opportunities.

"We have to get you to the studio at six tomorrow morning," Anthony said, snapping her out of her daydream.

"Okay," Christie whispered as she looked down.

Christie had been interviewed by many local reporters; including the exclusive interview she'd had with Janice to announce the release of her book. She was also scheduled for an interview with Good Morning America the next day.

Christie couldn't believe everything happening. She once sought understanding of the situation and now she wanted to share her story of that understanding with others. She glanced at her packed suitcases by the bedroom door and shifted in the rocking chair.

"Do you want me to take him?" Anthony asked as he held out his arms.

Christie didn't even need to look up before answering.

"No, I've got him," she replied as she looked down at the chubby brown bundle of joy in her arms. Christie marveled at how perfect he was. His skin was a cross between milk chocolate and pecan tan, his eyes were light brown and his hair lay perfectly on his scalp with a slight curl.

Christie was in love. For months after her father's death, she had battled nausea, weight-gain and countless other telltale signs. It wasn't until her blood test came back that Christie and Anthony found out the truth: They were pregnant.

Anthony leaned against the bedroom wall and watched his wife and son. Christie ran her finger across the baby's face and cooed at the same time he did.

"Isn't he perfect?" Christie asked.

They'd named him Kenneth after her father and he had arrived on a beautiful sunny day, a month before the trial began.

Baby Kenneth had been just the reminder that both Christie and Anthony needed. They had battled betrayal, backstabbing and lies but now had this ball of perfection to remind them life was still great.

Picking up his chunky arm, Christie smiled at the dangling bracelet, a replica of the charm necklace her father had given her.

"With him, now I have all the good luck I need. I don't have any more negativity around me and life just seems to be getting better by the day."

Anthony silently smiled as his heart warmed.

Christie often replayed her last conversation with her aunts that happened on the last day in the courthouse. She didn't remember much from the day but that conversation definitely stood out.

"You know…we never wanted it to come to this," Angelica had said quietly as they both stood waiting for an elevator. Christie acted as though she hadn't heard her aunt when Evelyn joined them and began talking in a hushed tone.

"At the end of the day, we're family, Christie."

Christie took this time to turn to both of her aunts and smile. She had too much to be thankful for—a baby waiting for her at home, a loving husband and a support system that rivaled most.

"You know, when I was little I wanted to be like both of you so much. I wanted to walk like you, Angelica, and I wanted to be tough like you, Evelyn," she said, nodding her head in their direction.

"But, now that I'm grown and have lived and experienced life, I'm thankful I'm not like you. I love you because we share the same blood but that's the extent of our relationship," she finished, reminding them of the letter they'd written to her.

Angelica and Evelyn stared at Christie as if they expected her to fall into their arms. She was a different person; she had changed. No longer down and out about their deception, she was ready to move beyond it.

As she sat holding baby Kenneth and reflecting over the past months, she couldn't stop beaming. Her publisher was projecting her book would become a New York Times Best Seller and she was already booked on several radio and television shows after its release.

Christie sighed as she cuddled her baby closer. The wounds she received from the deception of her family had been worth the pain and struggle. Not only had the situation showed her and everyone else that she had tough skin, but it also allowed her to begin to heal through telling her story.

"Who would've thought losing my daddy would put me on the path to do exactly what God destined me to do?" Christie asked, looking up at Anthony then down at Kenneth, the spitting image of her father.

Life wasn't perfect, but she was happy with what she'd been dealt; that's all she could ask for.

About the Author

Patrice Tartt is a hybrid of resiliency and passion topped off with cherry-on-top ambition. As a graduate of both Fisk University (B.A. in Psychology) and Trevecca Nazarene University (M.S. in Management), Patrice has always been motivated to reach higher levels while simultaneously motivating others to do the same. After dealing with the unexpected death of her father in 2011, Patrice was led to seek therapy through writing. Unknowingly, Patrice's therapeutic writing sessions led to the completion of her debut novel *Wounds of Deception,* which allowed her to tell a tangled story of hurt, anger and confusion while also healing. The Milwaukee, Wisconsin native, who is also an avid blogger and traveler, has a desire to educate and entertain through her writing- discussing seldom talked about topics like family betrayal, health issues, and the aftermath of pain- with a creative twist. Prior to becoming a published author, Patrice worked as an IT analyst and consultant. Patrice is an active member of Alpha Kappa Alpha Sorority, Incorporated, and currently resides in the Washington, D.C. metro area with her young son.